Editor-in-Chief and Founder:
Lyndon H. LaRouche, Jr.
Editorial Board: *Lyndon H. LaRouche, Jr. , Helga Zepp-LaRouche, Robert Ingraham, Tony Papert, Gerald Rose, Dennis Small, Jeffrey Steinberg, William Wertz*
Co-Editors: *Robert Ingraham, Tony Papert*
Technology: *Marsha Freeman*
Transcriptions: *Katherine Notley*
Ebooks: *Richard Burden*
Graphics: *Alan Yue*
Photos: *Stuart Lewis*
Circulation Manager: *Stanley Ezrol*

INTELLIGENCE DIRECTORS
Economics: *Marcia Merry Baker, Paul Gallagher*
History: *Anton Chaitkin*
Ibero-America: *Dennis Small*
Russia and Eastern Europe: *Rachel Douglas*
United States: *Debra Freeman*

INTERNATIONAL BUREAUS
Bogotá: *Miriam Redondo*
Berlin: *Rainer Apel*
Copenhagen: *Tom Gillesberg*
Lima: *Sara Madueño*
Melbourne: *Robert Barwick*
Mexico City: *Gerardo Castilleja Chávez*
New Delhi: *Ramtanu Maitra*
Paris: *Christine Bierre*
Stockholm: *Ulf Sandmark*
United Nations, N.Y.C.: *Leni Rubinstein*
Washington, D.C.: *William Jones*
Wiesbaden: *Göran Haglund*

ON THE WEB
e-mail: eirns@larouchepub.com
www.larouchepub.com
www.executiveintelligencereview.com
www.larouchepub.com/eiw
Webmaster: *John Sigerson*
Assistant Webmaster: *George Hollis*
Editor, Arabic-language edition: *Hussein Askary*

EIR (ISSN 0273-6314) *is published weekly (50 issues), by EIR News Service, Inc., P.O. Box 17390, Washington, D.C. 20041-0390. (703) 297-8434*

European Headquarters: E.I.R. GmbH, Postfach Bahnstrasse 9a, D-65205, Wiesbaden, Germany
Tel: 49-611-73650
Homepage: http://www.eir.de
e-mail: info@eir.de
Director: Georg Neudecker

Montreal, Canada: 514-461-1557
eir@eircanada.ca

Denmark: EIR - Danmark, Sankt Knuds Vej 11, basement left, DK-1903 Frederiksberg, Denmark.
Tel.: +45 35 43 60 40, Fax: +45 35 43 87 57. e-mail: eirdk@hotmail.com.

Mexico City: EIR, Sor Juana Inés de la Cruz 242-2 Col. Agricultura C.P. 11360
Delegación M. Hidalgo, México D.F.
Tel. (5525) 5318-2301
eirmexico@gmail.com

Canada Post Publication Sales Agreement #40683579

Postmaster: Send all address changes to *EIR*, P.O. Box 17390, Washington, D.C. 20041-0390.

Signed articles in *EIR* represent the views of the authors, and not necessarily those of the Editorial Board.

Four-Power Agreement for a New Bretton Woods

The American People's Rendezvous with History

by Bill Roberts in Detroit

Aug. 5—For many among those Americans only now confronting the reality of the philosophical fight encompassing the last 70 odd years of global history, this sudden rendezvous with history is nothing short of bewildering. The unravelling of the plot—by British MI6 intelligence, and Obama CIA chief John Brennan and other Obama loyal minions—to topple the duly elected president of the United States, has opened before the eyes of patriotic Americans a significantly broader image of the world they have in fact been living in all along.

Among President Trump's loyal base of supporters, the sense of commitment to defend the President, especially on matters of brokering peace agreements, has been solidified. In many respects, thanks in large degree to the work of the LaRouche Political Movement, the fascist coup against the President has backfired. The fake newscasters were beside themselves, lamenting the cheers Trump received at a campaign rally in Pennsylvania, when he expressed pleasure at how well his meeting with President Vladimir Putin had gone. They were furious that Trump seemed to side with Putin over the FBI on questions of election meddling. They even attempted to claim that the content of the discussion between the two Presidents was being entirely withheld from the American public— further evidence of Trump's nefarious plotting with the Russian enemy.

However, continued efforts to stymie future meetings between the two leaders, (much of the intention of Special Counsel Robert Mueller's witch-hunt against the President) seem to be failing. President Putin has been invited to meet with Trump in the oval office some time after the end of the year. In a recent poll, more than half of the American population is estimated to support plans for a second Trump-Putin summit.

While this political support among Trump's base (fully in opposition to the fraud known as Russiagate) is in full swing against efforts to assemble an impeachment-oriented Democratic majority in the U.S. Congress, it is not yet mobilized to support dismantling of the Wall Street derivatives bubble, a ticking time-bomb just as dangerous to the functioning of the Presidency as election of the pro-impeachment Democrats. There is also not an effective comprehension yet among the pro-Trump electorate, of why strengthening the U.S. relationship with China and Russia is so vitally important to the future of the world economy. These are obvious factors inhibiting President Trump from breaking, in a more meaningful way, from the very U.S.-British "special relationship" which he has in fact broken with over the defense of U.S. manufacturing and in his rejecting further regime-change wars.

Certain fissures in the ideological edifice, however, suggest the potential to break open further meaningful fights over principle: President Trump has effectively declared war on one of the biggest donors to Republican congressional candidates, the pro-drug legalization, pro-free trade, libertarian billionaire Charles Koch, who has broken profile and begun supporting Democratic Congressional candidates whose Republican opponents are too close to Trump on matters of free trade and presumably other policies. Meanwhile, this past week, Fox Business operated as a platform for individuals inside and outside the Trump Administration, pressuring Trump to move to escalate tariffs against China rather than making concessions in the name of good faith and mutual benefit.

At political tables in the streets and at campaign events, the LaRouche PAC is effectively confronting the American people with their own designated role in history. Not their role in an election, not passively "supporting" or voting, nor in saying they are for this or that, but in recognizing their place in an on-going process of history for which they are responsible.

What confronts the American people now, is the fact that the coup organized against President Trump is now shown to have been created by assets of British MI6 Intelligence and Britain's GCHQ, the same malefactors who gave us the "dodgy dossier" on Iraqi weapons of mass destruction. This means that these operations against the President are being done in defense of the British Empire's war policy, and in defense of those networks who have dutifully organized U.S. policy on the British Empire's behalf.

What further confronts the American people is the historical fact that the primary figure leading the fight against British Empire policy for forty-plus years, in favor of actual sovereign U.S. interests, is Lyndon LaRouche, the only other individual in recent U.S. history to incur the full wrath of the protectors of the U.S.-British special relationship, including legal assassin Robert Mueller. It was LaRouche who opposed the United States' becoming a financial services economy, urging us to instead produce capital goods for the development of the third world, and to commit to cooperation for the common aims of mankind and end the threat of nuclear war.

Realizing that what is at stake is the actual, decades-long fight against the historic enemy of the nation, intersecting as it does the current operations to subvert the U.S. Presidency, places the average American on the stage of history in a way that makes squirming away from responsibility, in favor of issue-based ideological comfort-zones, increasingly difficult.

BRICS: Work Still To Be Done To Defeat the British Empire

by Ramasimong Phillip Tsokolibane

Aug. 4—One can only be encouraged by the proceedings at the recently concluded 10th BRICS summit in Johannesburg, chaired by our nation. What we saw in statements from the gathered Heads of State, and including China's President Xi Jinping and Russia's President Vladimir Putin—altogether representing nearly half of the world's population—was strikingly different from the blathering bullshit that characterizes the gatherings of the institutions of the dying old paradigm of the British Empire's globalized monetarist system. Instead, there was the kind of serious deliberation on a pathway for peace and development that will constitute the content of the New Global Paradigm. Unique also was the attention and respect paid to the developing nations of the South, including the entire African continent, which was not the kind of master-to-slave diktats that come from the likes of the IMF.

Looking into the future, the BRICS member nations and their strategic partners see the possibilities for growth, peace and prosperity that a developing Africa brings, and have stated their commitment to take steps with investment in both social and physical infrastructure, in industry, and in strengthening what binds us together—our creative human potential. As President Xi so ably stated, they do this not for strategic or monetary gain, but because it is right to do so. Following the teachings of Confucius, and the best of Western religions, enrichment of your neighbor's life, enriches your own. An essential characteristic of the New Paradigm is a determination to eliminate the zero-sum games of British monetarism,

EDITORIAL

and to act on policies directed at creating only winners.

I applaud this message of hope for a future without losers, with freedom from the Hobbesian markets, which have crushed humanity under plodding boots. It is something that my movement, and its leaders Lyndon and Helga LaRouche, have fought for tirelessly for more than a half-century, and at great risk to their persons, against the bitch Queen of the British Empire and her lackeys and managers. We stand on the edge of an historic victory for all mankind.

But I must add a word of caution to those who might think that the battle is won. The British Empire will not simply yield to the force of history and concede the oligarchical power that has driven its policies to litter the world with billions of bodies over the last century. The truth and power of the new ideas represented by the New Paradigm, which seeks peace, prosperity and progress for all of mankind, can eventually win out, but not without a struggle, which may indeed get pretty nasty, and even bloodier with the forces of evil surrounding the bitch Queen and her Empire. It is our job to give force and direction to this fight, to identify the weaknesses in our enemy and to expose the Imperial traitors to our nations and to human progress itself.

I have attempted to do that in my exposure of the work of the Queen's lackey, the former President of the United States, Barack Obama, in recruiting a global movement against the BRICS, and especially against its leading nations, China and Russia. Obama gave the keynote to this anti-BRICS initiative in his July 17

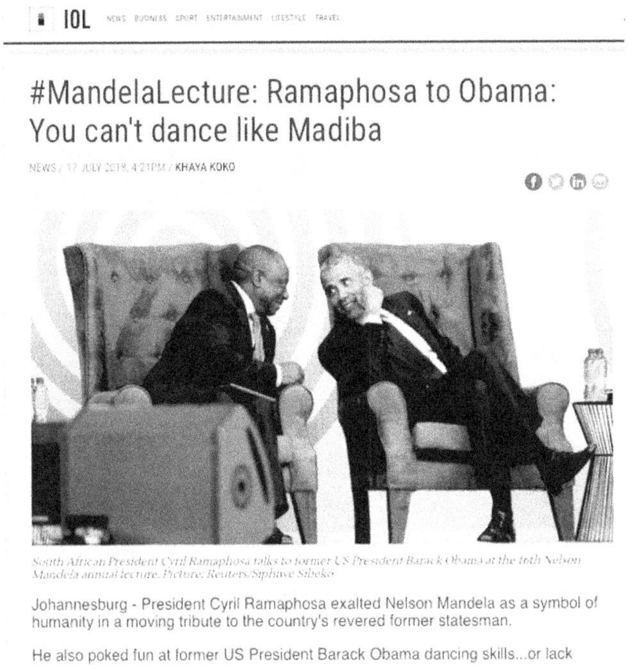

South African President Cyril Ramaphosa talks to former US President Barack Obama at the 16th Nelson Mandela annual lecture. Picture: Reuters/Siphiwe Sibeko

Johannesburg - President Cyril Ramaphosa exalted Nelson Mandela as a symbol of humanity in a moving tribute to the country's revered former statesman.

He also poked fun at former US President Barack Obama dancing skills...or lack

Annual Mandela Lecture that desecrated the memory of our nation's father, Nelson Mandela. He falsely claimed that the Chinese model for economic development is dangerous because it is autocratic and denies individual human freedom, and therefore must be rejected by Africa and the rest of the world.

Instead he argued for the total freedom of the markets, even if those markets would cause Africa to be left without funding for large projects. Progress and freedom, this evil lawn jockey claimed, is best served by looking inward, and not in some globally expansive and overly expensive scheme. Reject the lure of easy money offered by the Chinese, said Obama, and by implication, the development plans offered by the Russians as well, because they seek to enslave you to their debt.

As the BRICS conference moved towards its close, Obama's line has been picked up all over the world, promoted by the propaganda arm of the British Empire—what the embattled American President Donald Trump has correctly labeled the "fake news media." Unfortunately, this lie was also repeated in a paper titled "China's Trade-Disruptive Economic Model" at the July 26 World Trade Organization (WTO) General Council meeting in Geneva by Dennis Shea, President Trump's appointed Ambassador to the WTO.

Bring In the New Paradigm

I need to make something very clear. The lending practices of China, Russia, and the New Development Bank (NDB, an arm of the BRICS) are strikingly different from those of the financial institutions of the dying empire of money of the City of London and Wall Street. Whereas China, Russia and the NDB are issuing credit for a purpose—for specific development and other projects—without regard to making financial profit on what is lent, what little lending emanates from Wall Street and the City of London is for *profit*, that is, to make money—financial profit—for the lender, as much as they can extract, even if that means the creation of conditions that will kill large numbers of people.

This is nothing new: Shakespeare had accurately characterized the Venetian lender, Shylock, as seeking his "pound of flesh." That play is called *The Merchant of Venice* and it takes place in the devil's own city-state that gave birth to the modern form of the monetarist system, and whose spores created the British Empire and the City of London.

Regardless of what the BRICS leaders—including President Xi—say about not intending to pose a challenge to the existing, globalized monetarist system, this concept of "credit for purpose, not for profit" is the most serious challenge to that system in its present incarnation. It parallels the ideas of the great American Treasury Secretary Alexander Hamilton, and of Lyndon LaRouche. With nations representing nearly half the world's population acting within a new system of credit that is coming into being, I can tell you, the bitch Queen is not amused.

The BRICS represents the seed crystal for this new system. I urge its leadership to act both consciously and decisively to bring the New Paradigm into reality as quickly as possible. An international conference could be convened immediately, just as Helga Zepp-LaRouche has called for, which will go beyond what was done at the 1944 Bretton Woods Conference, to create a new financial infrastructure suitable for the distribution of vast amounts of credit for long-term infrastructure construction, and other projects, and which will return the world to a stable relationship among national currencies, ending the wild, casino-like speculation of the current system.

This new system will *replace* the discredited and hated International Monetary Fund and a World

Bank whose flawed and restrictive charter has always prevented it from lending for any large projects, such as those envisioned in China's Belt and Road Initiative. To state it again: *We cannot reform the old system.* We need a new one, one that creates stability and promotes the creation of massive amounts of Hamiltonian/China modeled credit, without regard for monetarist profit.

Such a conference and such an outcome need to be accomplished as quickly as possible, before the British try to blow up the long-ago collapsed existing system, kept alive with transfusions of trillions of dollars sucked into the City of London/Wall Street casino. There is talk in the media about blowing up the system sometime in the next few weeks, prior to important mid-term elections in the USA, in order to turn support away from their strategic adversary, the economic-policy challenged President Trump.

Trump is not Africa's enemy, as some stupid people on the continent and in South Africa contend. Rather, it is the British Empire and the London/Wall Street axis, which Trump often challenges, that remains the enemy of all mankind. As I have said before, President Trump and the United States should ask to join the BRICS and the United States should bring itself into the New Paradigm. "This will never happen," you say? "The U.S. will never be a force for progress!" Not only can this happen—we must make it happen.

Workers at the new First Automotive Works (FAW) Group assembly plant, built by China in Nelson Mandela Bay Municipality, South Africa, July 10, 2014.

We have, as they say, a lot of heavy lifting to do, to rapidly bring the New Paradigm into being. Much of our government and national leadership are both fakers and liars. We saw our President hug the BRICS leaders and seem to embrace their policies. But we saw that same Cyril Ramaphosa only a few days earlier hug Obama, and praise him. And didn't we see him, a couple of weeks ago, in London, getting orders from his true masters?

We must finally create, here and everywhere, a new leadership, committed to progress for all of mankind. Take off the blinders that have been put on us by the fake media and the likes of the lawn jockey Obama, and take responsibility for our future, for the sake of all our citizens and all of Africa. Onward to our true destiny! Will you join me?

Rogers Vows to Eliminate Poverty in U.S.A. by 2030

by Stephanie Ezrol

Aug. 3—Kesha Rogers, an Independent candidate for Congress in Texas's 9th CD, has vowed to lead a drive to eliminate poverty in the United States by 2030 if she is elected to Congress. In a statement issued by her campaign last week, she said that "by re-establishing our own economic sovereignty over Wall Street, we can use the Constitutional mechanisms to fund our own recovery through a Hamiltonian credit system, and eliminate poverty in the United States by 2030. If we fully unleashed the power of our unique Constitutional system, and collaborated with China and Russia in the Belt and Road Initiative with the determination" that Martin Luther King so strongly stood for, we could end poverty in the United States and for everyone on Earth by 2050.

We reached Rogers between campaign events and were able to briefly discuss her ambitious approach, which is certainly a breath of fresh air in today's jaded political environment, in which most candidates have hardened their hearts to human suffering whether it be in America's inner cities, in our largely deindustrialized industrial Mid-West, or regions still not repaired from Hurricanes Katrina,

Kesha Rogers

Sandy and Harvey, or in war-torn and drug-infested regions of the world from Mexico to Yemen to Afghanistan, to name just a few of the heart-wrenching crisis spots in the world. Rogers looks to a uniquely American approach, one that she sees echoed in China's Belt and Road Initiative.

She doesn't mince words: "America's great industrial productivity and the U.S. economy have been in an ongoing collapse, and continue to be dominated by the geopolitical, anti-growth policies of Wall Street and London's monetary empire. Now, the poorest areas of our nation, once blooming in great industrial, manufacturing and agricultural development, have been driven into the scrap heap. The United States suffers from extreme rates of poverty, suicide, drug abuse, a decline in basic economic infrastructure, and a lack of savings and funding for the future."

The American Anti-Colonial Heritage

Rogers sees China moving in a different direction, an approach that she sees as harking back to America's Presidents Franklin Delano Roosevelt and John Kennedy. She points to what she calls China's "economic miracle for poverty alleviation, lifting hundreds of millions out of poverty with targeted projects and strategies that address the unique problems of each town. This hasn't just worked in China, but all across the world, most notably in Africa."

She heralds America's anti-colonial heritage that she sees as critical to ending poverty not only in the United States but in the world as a whole. Again she goes to the strategic approach of China that is becoming more and more the realization of the best of the American tradition. The China-Africa collaboration is a paradigm we can, and must, learn from, according to Rogers. Her just released campaign statement underscores "the rapid development of the physical economy" now underway in Africa accomplished by "building rail development corridors, and modernizing ports." That Chinese win-win policy she says, "is now undoing the deliberate policies of colonialism, wars, and economic ruin, of the British Empire."

China is using the Hamiltonian credit system, referring to the unique anti-monetarist credit policies of America's first Treasury Secretary, Alexander Hamilton. "China has begun financing and directing the building of all kinds of projects across the continent of Africa, linking nations economically. This includes connecting highways, railroads, and waterways across the entire continent, replenishing Lake Chad, building

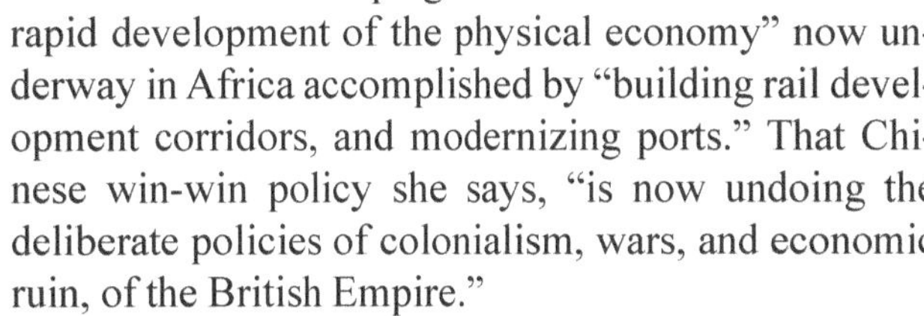

new dams, power plants, and farms with advanced crop science, and building basic infrastructure like hospitals, schools, and markets.

"Contrary to allegations of land-grabbing African natural resources, the activity of Chinese firms is focused on production to meet the growing demand in Africa itself," not the rip-everything-out colonial style looting that merely grabs raw materials from Africa. This Chinese approach, which most readers of *EIR* are quite familiar with, is the direct opposite of the British, French, Belgian and other colonial looting of Africa, be it in the so-called colonial era or the more modern era under Queen Elizabeth II's consort Prince Philip's World Wildlife Fund.

Rogers told *EIR* that she believes it is extremely important for the American people to look at what China is really doing in Africa and not be bamboozled by the stories from the fake media and their xenophobic talking heads on television, radio and the Internet. China, by its domestic poverty alleviation measures and its projects in Africa, provides a "model for the United States in alleviating poverty" in what she calls our "deliberately created ghettos." What many African nations are doing now in cooperation with China and the BRICS nations, Rogers advocates, "must be adopted in the United States to transform our neglected communities ruined by criminal negligence" into prosperity for all people, not for the few alone.

One Size Does Not Fit All

The key, she stressed to this reporter, is breaking out of the colonial looting mindset, whether it be Enron style corporate looting, financial speculation, or the endless wars we have suffered through under Bush-Cheney and Obama. She said that one of the biggest concerns of her campaign is the issue of poverty, which is rampant among African-Americans and other minority communities in her district. She wants to get people to see that there are solutions. The Chinese approach of building new infrastructure, energy production and manufacturing all over the planet is uniquely people-centered. She finds this to be a critical element, saying: "Real poverty alleviation means figuring out the unique requirements of an area, and unique skills of its population, and responding to these needs specifically, rather than a one size fits all approach, similar to what President Franklin Roosevelt did with the Tennessee Valley Authority."

Rogers, a long time student of the LaRouche-Riemann method of economic forecasting, reminded this reporter that people are our most valuable resource. "Consider a few of the cities of the United States which are currently desperately impoverished, including right here in Texas. Aren't nearly all of them on rivers or coastlines, near formerly highly productive manufacturing centers? If the United States were to join with China in the Belt and Road Initiative, aren't these cities the precise locations which would have to be brought back to life, with modern deep water ports, container docks, and high-speed rail? Think about the positive impact that this would have on the African-American population of the United States, for example, which still has double and triple the death rates of the non-African-American or Hispanic population."

Rogers is very happy about the sea change she sees happening in the world. She has boldly told her constituents, "The mutually profitable relationship between China and countries in Africa is the same type of win-win relationship we can expect if the United States accepts China's offer to participate in the Belt and Road Initiative."

Trump's Positive Peace Initiatives

The candidate sees great hope in President Trump's peace initiatives, saying, he "has dedicated himself to restoring and expanding the decayed U.S. infrastructure, and increasing positive relations with Russia and China as well as other leading nations around the world." She emphasized that Trump's "commitment to abolishing the imperial policies of the British Empire and ushering in a new paradigm of economic progress is one that has been the continued mission for the last 40-plus years of American Statesman Lyndon LaRouche, along with his wife Helga."

Rogers knows she can't do it alone. As she stated at the outset of her discussion with this author, she intends to lead a drive to eliminate poverty. Her statement hits the point quite concisely saying, "We need leaders in U.S. Congress who will fight to bring the United States on board the new paradigm transforming the planet. That means putting an end to the ruinous systems of IMF, Wall Street and City of London monetary control, and implementing the needed American System credit solutions that have been the driver of our nation's economic growth, exemplified under Presidents like Lincoln, Franklin Roosevelt, and John F. Kennedy. She concluded her discussion with *EIR* saying, "We are being left behind. What are we waiting for? We have to step outside of U.S. internal affairs, and see where the solutions to poverty are already in play."

EIR Contents

www.larouchepub.com   Volume 45, Number 32, August 10, 2018

The Four Powers

illustration by Chance McGee

Trump and Conte Launch U.S.-Italy Preferential Relationship

by Claudio Celani

Aug. 7—At their meeting in Washington on July 30, President Trump and Italian Prime Minister Antonio Conte launched a "preferential relationship" which goes beyond the mere affinities among so-called "populist" governments. The historical reference here is to the alliance between Italy and the U.S. sought by Enrico Mattei after the 1956 Suez Crisis, when Italy was the only European country to vote in support of the U.S. resolution condemning France and Britain for invading Egypt. Eventually, Mattei's efforts were successful under the Kennedy Administration and Aldo Moro. (See *EIR*, June 5, 2009: "Mattei and Kennedy: The Strategic Alliance Killed by the British").

White House/Stephanie Chasez

President Trump welcomes Italian Prime Minister Conte to the White House on July 30, 2018.

The current U.S. and Italian governments are expressions of the voters' reactions against the same neo-colonial forces, including the European Union, which in recent times have brought us "regime change" wars in the North African/Middle Eastern theater and, through their bankrupt economic policies, have produced deindustrialization, unemployment and poverty.

Prime Minister Conte was greeted by a LaRouche PAC welcoming committee on his arrival at the White House. LPAC organizers displayed a large banner saying "Benvenuto Prime Minister Conte—Go Glass-Steagall!"—referring to the financial reform contained in the Italian government program. Conte waved at the sight of the banner, which was covered by some Italian news agencies.

At the joint press conference of the two leaders, President Trump stated that the United States recognizes Italy's leadership role in the Mediterranean, while Italian Prime Minister Conte announced that a joint U.S.-Italy "steering committee" has been established to stabilize Libya, confirming what he had previously said on background to a group of Italian journalists.

The new "axis" between Italy and the Trump Administration has freaked out the EU establishment. Exemplary is a July 31 commentary in Germany's *Die Welt*: "Conte is now Trump's man in Europe. His best friend on a continent which he just called an enemy. A new axis seems to have been born: Washington-Rome. It will stand against the old Berlin-Paris axis. 'We are now partners,' Trump said. It is a partnership against the dominance of Germany and France, of Angela Merkel and Emmanuel Macron," *Die Welt* wrote.

The German liberal daily is correct: Italy and the USA are building a partnership against the old Berlin-Paris axis. However, the Berlin-Paris axis is no longer what it was when it was founded under De Gaulle and Adenauer. Then it was a partnership between two countries seeking the "benefit of the other" and the well-being of their own populations, but it has transformed itself into its opposite under the influence of the City of London.

In this respect, Rome's choice to decouple itself *de facto*, albeit not yet formally, from the Franco-German dominated EU and seek the backing of a powerful ally in the USA, has no ideological color. It is not only Ma-

The LaRouche Political Action Committee rallies in support of Italian Prime Minister Conte. Washington, D.C., July 31, 2018.

chiavellian in its highest meaning, but can and must be seen as the beginning of a liberation war.

Both Trump and Conte had stressed the significance of their bilateral relations in their joint press conference.

Trump said, "Today, Prime Minister Conte and I are pleased to announce a new strategic dialogue between Italy and the United States that will enhance cooperation on a range of issues. This includes joint security efforts in the Mediterranean, where we recognize Italy's leadership role in the stabilization of Libya and North Africa."

Conte said that both parties had agreed to set up a "steering committee … in the Mediterranean between Italy and the United States. I would say that we're almost twin countries, in which Italy is becoming a reference point in Europe and a privileged interlocutor for the United States, for the main threats and challenges that we have before us—terrorism—and for all the crises that we see in the Mediterranean and, in particular, in regards to Libya.

"Secondly, the American administration also recognizes that Italy has a leadership role as a promoter country that will lead to the stabilization of Libya. And of course, this with great respect for the Libyan population."

Later, Conte announced that "we are going to organize, in agreement with President Trump—I'm going to organize a conference on Libya. We would like to deal with and discuss all of the issues relating to the Libyan people, involving all of the stakeholders, actors, and protagonists in the whole of the Mediterranean. We are going to discuss economic aspects but also social aspects; the protection of civil rights; the problem of constitutional process, of issuing and passing laws [inau-

dible] to enable Libya in particular to get to democratic elections in a condition of the utmost stability."

Conte also announced the development of a commercial spaceplane as a joint U.S.-Italian industrial project. "I personally am sure that we can increase and improve the relationship with the United States at all levels, and in particular, in the space and aerospace fields. We already have a great partnership between the Italian Space Agency and NASA, so we hope that aerospace will bring together American technology and Italian technology, so that we can launch a new aircraft that will cross the atmosphere, and will be able to bring the United States and Italy together in an hour and a half.

"This is a project that I'd like to discuss in detail with the American administration," he said.

Italy is currently developing the Space Rider project, a sub-orbital re-entry vehicle which needs a rocket launcher to reach about a 400 km (240 mile) altitude, and has an agreement with Virgin Galactic to participate in the development of Virgin's own spaceplane.

Whereas these projects rely on existing technologies, a real breakthrough would be the development of a "scramjet," a hypersonic plane in which engine combustion takes place in hypersonic airflow. Italy has a great tradition in scramjet research through Antonio Ferri, who first worked in the first-ever supersonic wind tunnel in 1937-40 in Italy, and later, in the U.S., pioneered groundbreaking research on hypersonic thermofluid dynamics.

Italy/France Contradictions Over Libya

Stabilizing Libya is of utmost importance for Italy, both on commercial (Italy imports 23% of its oil and 10% of its gas from Libya) and security grounds. Libya is the main base for the human traffickers who organize mass illegal immigration through the Mediterranean, and it harbors ISIS or ISIS-allied groups which are a potential terrorist threat.

The main responsibility for the chaos in Libya rests on former French President Nicolas Sarkozy, who launched the war against Libya in 2011. France has never apologized to Italy for today's refugee waves, but on the contrary, has hampered Italian attempts to share the burden. This took spectacular dimensions when

Emmanuel Macron, French Prime Minister (far right), and Federica Mogherini, High Representative of the European Union for Foreign Affairs and Security Policy (center), with other participants at the International Conference on Libya, at the Elysée Palace in Paris, France, May 29, 2018.

President Macron's party spokesperson characterized the Italian decision not to let an NGO refugee ship enter Italian ports as "nauseating."

Previous Italian governments, while they saw the French attempts to expand its sphere of influence in North Africa, did not challenge them lest they break the hypocritical "European consensus." But the current government has decided to draw a red line and act on its own initiative.

Thus, when Emmanuel Macron, without consulting his EU allies, convened a summit of Libyan rival leaders in Paris last May 29, and had them agree on a schedule for presidential elections, Rome decided it was time to act.

Last July, three members of the Italian government visited Tripoli: Interior Minister Salvini, Foreign Minister Moavero and, on July 24, Defense Minister Elisabetta Trenta. During her meeting with Fayez al-Serraj, the Prime Minister of Libya recognized by the UN, Trenta said Italy opposes the holding of elections next Dec. 10 as agreed with Macron. "I believe that the reconciliation process in Libya must be inclusive," Trenta said in the meeting with Serraj. "Therefore, I think that talking about new elections before completing such a process is a mistake. Afterwards, we would still have the same problems, in Italy as well as in Libya."

During Trenta's visit to Tripoli, local media reported that France intends to establish a military base in Libya, a report that was confirmed to *Huffington Post Italia* by Tripoli government sources.

Italy has now resumed the friendship and coopera-

tion treaty signed by then-Prime Minister Berlusconi with Qaddafi in 2009, which includes Italian investments in roads, hospitals, etc., as a compensation for the colonial period. In addition, Rome has provided Tripoli's coast guard with twelve patrol ships to be able to control its sea borders.

Rome has so far had privileged relations with the UN-recognized government in Tripoli, but it intends to also involve Serraj's rival, General Khalifa Haftar, the head of the Libyan National Army, who controls the eastern part of the country. Defense Minister Trenta said that she will soon meet Haftar. Interior Minister Salvini's recent meeting with Egyptian President Al Sisi, Haftar's main sponsor, goes in the same direction.

Also, Trenta was reported in the media as giving "full support to the process of unification of the armed forces, a process that must involve all security players who want to participate in the defense of the state. The monopoly of force must belong to the state."

This complements the conditions demanded by Haftar and the Tobruk parliament, and opposed by armed militias, including some militias currently backing Serraj.

The Tripoli government recently joined the Belt and Road Initiative, a decision which was welcomed in Rome because it offers a development perspective for reconciliation.

Italy Under ECB/EU Blackmail

The second front where Washington could help Italy is the economic/financial situation. The Conte government wants to pull the Italian economy out of years of stagnation with a modest investment program, but it is facing EU opposition. EU rules do not allow deficit spending, and therefore Italy is facing a confrontation with the EU on the budget. In addition, in five months the ECB will suspend its Assets Purchase Program (resembling "quantitative easing"), and in many circles nervousness and speculation is increasing on how the Italian "populist" government will react to a new bond crisis. Especially in Germany, fears are growing that in the worst case scenario, Italy won't honor its "Target 2" liabilities, whose main creditor is the Bundesbank.

Target 2 is a clearing system inside the Eurosystem, the system of euro-area central banks, and is a fraud in and of itself. Under the Target 2 system, the European

Central Bank (ECB) buys government bonds from banks. The banks are accounted a credit at the ECB (i.e. money), but the ECB places an equal liability on the account of the national central bank of the nominal assets. In other words, the ECB acts as a foreign bank to all members of the Eurosystem. No other central bank in the world acts like that. It is as though the Federal Reserve, which also purchases assets by issuing liquidity, demanded that someone else cover the costs.

Under Target 2, the Bundesbank has accumulated the highest credit towards the ECB: 976 billion euros, and the Bank of Italy the highest debt at 465 billion.

Some German economists, such as Thomas Mayer from the Flossbach von Storch Research Institute, and Clemens Fuest of the IFO institute, are spreading the fear that in the end, since countries such as Italy will not be able to foot the bill, either the Bundesbank will never see that money, or else there will be a big writedown. Instead, they propose that the Bundesbank unilaterally withdraw from the Target 2 system.

In reality, if such accounts ever do have to be balanced, the central bank with the liability can always sell the bonds in order to pay the bill—probably at a loss because the value of such assets would fall, but in the case of exiting the Euro, this could be done with a relatively minor issue of national currency.

The question is complicated and weird enough so that public opinion gets confused by opposing propaganda, especially because everything is discussed from the monetarist standpoint of money as value-in-itself. The most important rumors flow from the City of London, where the bulk of the speculation on these scenarios takes place. But it is a reflex of the preparations for the big crisis ready to explode at the end of the year.

On the other side, the Italian daily *Corriere della Sera* has reported rumors that Italian Treasury Minister Giovanni Tria is planning to visit China to discuss the possibility that Beijing might help sustain the Italian government debt after the end of ECB purchases. This has not been confirmed, but it is plausible because Tria has good connections with China.

Someone should suggest to Tria a scheme to have the

Giovanni Tria, Italian Minister of Economy and Finances.

Chinese buy Italian debt, and re-invest it in a newly created Bank for Infrastructural Investments, to finance for instance the infrastructure in Southern Italy which the Chinese already wanted to build in 2011, but which were vetoed by the EU and by Hillary Clinton.

The Domestic Fifth Column

As if it were not enough to have so many friendly enemies in the EU, the new Italian government has a fifth column inside it, represented by the radical anti-growth faction of the Five Star Movement (M5S). The Five Star has always campaigned against big infrastructure, such as the Turin-Lyon high-speed line (TAV) which is under construction, or the Trans-Adriatic Pipeline (TAP), which is intended to carry gas from Azerbaijan to Southern Italy. Some of the leading activists against such projects are now in the government, such as Transport and Infrastructure Minister Danilo Toninelli, or Mezzogiorno Minister Barbara Lezzi. A brawl has now broken out in the government between those two M5S representatives and their Lega coalition partners, as Toninelli and Lezzi have called for stopping TAV and TAP, while the Lega, through its leader Matteo Salvini, said the projects should go on.

To stop the Turin-Lyon TAV would be suicidal for Italy. It is essential to connect the port of Genoa, which has been identified as one terminal of the Maritime Silk Road, with the Trans-European Corridors 3 (Lisbon-Kiev) and 5 (Rotterdam-Genoa). Connections already exist, but they are obsolete as concerns speed and capacity. For instance, the current Turin-Lyon line goes through a tunnel that was built in the nineteenth century, and does not accommodate modern container size.

Another project under construction, the "Third Pass," is also opposed by the M5S. This is a new line, parallel to the existing one, going from Genoa through the Appennine Mountains to the Piedmont and Lombardy regions, intersecting the already-mentioned Corridor 3 and completing Corridor 5.

If Prime Minister Conte and others do not succeed in solving the conflict, this might even bring down the government, to the delight of Brussels, Paris and Frankfurt—and London.

India-Pakistan: Regional Developments Shine a Glimmer of Hope for Real Peace

by Ramtanu Maitra

Aug. 4—The depth of animosity and mistrust that has dominated India-Pakistan relations over the decades exasperated international political observers long ago, and most have concluded that establishment of peace between India and Pakistan is virtually impossible. In degrees of difficulty, the task perhaps rests on a par with that of establishing peace between the Israelis and Palestinians, and is considered a generous notch above landing astronauts on the Moon.

However, notwithstanding such apparently insurmountable difficulty, it is evident that peace between India and Pakistan would not only serve both countries well, but would also enhance the security of the now-developing Eurasian region.

As of now, there is no indication that authorities in either Islamabad, or New Delhi, are deeply involved in working out measures for an all-around peace between the two countries as one of their urgent priorities. Yet, there may be a glimmer of hope on the horizon in light of some changes that have taken place in the region. And that includes the change of guard in Islamabad through its National Assembly elections last month. Although the new Prime Minister, Imran Khan, leading the Khyber Pakhtunkhwa-based Pakistan Tehrik-e-Insaf (PTI), has not formed his coalition government at the time this article was written, media reports indicate he has the support of Pakistan's all-powerful military. That could be a positive factor, if, and when, efforts are made to establish a meaningful peace between the two countries.

To carefully assess the potential for progress in Indo-Pakistani relations today, it is first necessary to set the context.

The British Colonial Curse

The seven-decade-old animosity between India and Pakistan began in 1947, on the very day the British Raj left the subcontinent after almost 300 years of the divide-and-rule policy that sharpened the division between subcontinent's two major religious groups, Hindus and Muslims. As a departing kick, British officials drew the borders in 40 days, using out-of-date maps and dated census materials to partition the subcontinent on the basis of religious demography, thus creating within it a nation for the Muslims—Pakistan—in two parts, East and West, separated by about 1,000 miles of Indian territory.

Having thus plunged the entire subcontinent into chaos and violence, the departing colonials handed

Refugee trains bringing Muslims from India to Pakistan, and Hindus from Pakistan to India during Partition in 1947.

over the reins to newly formed India and Pakistan. Compounding the chaos, the colonials left 565 independent princely states, whose lands comprised two-fifths of the subcontinent with a population 99 million at the time. The rulers of these princely states were given the option to join either India or Pakistan.

The violent riots between Hindus and Muslims that the British had nurtured to break up the subcontinent, got worse following the partition, and began to metamorphose from hostility between the Hindus and Muslims into that between India and Pakistan—not altogether an unexpected fall-out, since one of the nations was formed for people belonging to a particular religion. Israelis and Palestinians, or Irishmen for that matter, well know the type of conflict that carving out a religious state from the body of a country sparks and perpetuates.

Neither should it have been surprising that this state of impassioned chaos was quickly transformed into full-fledged war between the two new nations. One of the princely states, situated between India and Pakistan in the north, Jammu and Kashmir, became the first major battlefield. In October 1947, Pushtun tribesmen, accompanied by Pakistani troops wearing the garb of tribesmen from Pakistan's North-West Frontier Province (renamed Khyber Pakhtunkhwa by Islamabad in 2010), invaded the state of Jammu and Kashmir. Troubled by the increasing deterioration in law and order and by earlier raids, which culminated in the invasion of the "tribesmen," the ruler of Jammu and Kashmir, Maharaja Hari Singh, signed the Instrument of Accession to merge the state with India, and requested armed assistance from India.

Indian troops stopped the Pakistani troops from advancing, but did not push them back to where they had come from. Thus the divided and disputed state of Jammu and

Kashmir was born. Since Islamabad did not recognize the Instrument of Accession, it continues to claim that the state belongs to Pakistan on the basis of its Muslim majority; and for years, Islamabad has deployed well-armed terrorists to weaken Indian control there.

Since that first war over the state of Jammu and Kashmir in 1947, animosity has become more pronounced. India and Pakistan have fought two more wars—the last, in 1971, resulted in the separation of Pakistan's eastern wing from its western wing to become an independent nation-state, Bangladesh.

Beyond Simla: How Pakistani Terrorism Was Born

Following the 1971 war, on July 2, 1972, the late Indian Prime Minister Indira Gandhi and the late Pakistani President Zulfikar Ali Bhutto signed the Simla Agreement. It begins thus:

> The Government of India and the Government of Pakistan are resolved that the two countries put an end to the conflict and confrontation that have hitherto marred their relations and work for the promotion of a friendly and harmonious relationship and the establishment of durable peace in the subcontinent so that both countries may henceforth devote their resources and energies to the pressing task of advancing the welfare of their people. (Ministry of External Affairs, Government of India, *Simla Agreement,* July 2, 1972)

On the status of the state of Jammu and Kashmir, the agreement states:

> The line of control resulting from the ceasefire of December 17, 1971, shall be respected by both

Sir Hari Singh, Maharaja of Jammu and Kashmir, in 1944.

sides without prejudice to the recognized position of either side. Neither side shall seek to alter it unilaterally, irrespective of mutual differences and legal interpretations. Both sides further undertake to refrain from the threat or the use of force in violation of this line.

The Cold War greatly strengthened the Pakistani military's hand. Pakistan was an important geopolitical ally to undermine the Soviets and their allies, including India. Beholden to Saudi Arabia, Britain, and the United States, the Pakistani military was "used" to serve the anti-Soviet "democrats" and Islamists. The Islamist mob was recruited, armed and provided guidance. Their alliance with the anti-India jihadis within Pakistan was viewed by the anti-Soviet West as a mere blip on the radar screen. The Soviet Union's invasion of Afghanistan in 1979, and its decade-long floundering there, allowed the West and the Saudis to build up Pakistan as a hub of armed orthodox Islamists who "hated" everyone with passion, including the Hindus of India.

At the same time, the British curse continued to plague India-Pakistan relations. Britain harbors politicians, bureaucrats, immigrants and Islamists who spare no effort to stoke the fires of the Kashmir conflict, organizing those who are ready to lay down their lives to establish an independent Kashmir. Even if such efforts

Bhutto.org

Pakistani President Zulfikar Ali Bhutto and Indian Prime Minister Indira Gandhi signing the Simla Agreement. Simla, India, July 2, 1972.

were met with little success, London's empire-servers needed the conflict to maintain its influence over the area and to prevent India and Pakistan from working together for the development of their respective countries. As a result of hundreds of years of involvement in the Indian subcontinent as colonial rulers, during which time they "educated" a stream of the Indian and Pakistani elite, London has assets on both sides of partitioned Kashmir. Some are old assets, who have kept the pot boiling all this while; and some are new, and decidedly more violent.

Understandably, the shadow of the past wars has made it difficult to push ahead with an admittedly feeble peace process. Still, efforts were made over the years; but, repeatedly sabotaged, those efforts failed to lay a firm foundation for a real peace process to mature.

Progress and Setbacks

A landmark date in efforts to lay the foundation for peace between the two countries was Feb. 21, 1999, when the Prime Ministers of the two countries— Atal Bihari Vajpayee of India and Mian Nawaz Sharif of Pakistan—signed the Lahore Declaration. This committed India and Pakistan to intensify their efforts to resolve all issues.

RIA Novosti/Yurii Somov

Soviet forces in Afghanistan in 1986.

swiss-image.ch/Remy Steinegger

Pervez Musharraf, President of Pakistan, speaking at the World Economic Forum, January 24, 2008.

CC/Deccan Herald

Atal Bihari Vajpayee, Indian Prime Minister, 1998-2004.

"cross-border terrorism" in the Kashmir Valley. In his breakfast meeting with Indian media, Musharraf said that the Kashmir dispute remained central to ending enmity with India. (Umbreen Javaid and Khushboo Ejaz, "The Agra Summit: A Critical Appraisal," June 2017) Within months, however, on Dec. 13, 2001, Pakistani terrorists attacked the Indian Parliament in New Delhi.

At that point, the prospect of resuming a fresh round of peace talks seemed unattainable. Nonetheless, the potential of a stalemate in the protracted crisis once again led the two sides to sit at a negotiating table in 2004. The resulting Composite Dialogue lasted for five years, during which public diplomatic gestures by Indian and Pakistani leaders facilitated discussion and softened attitudes among civil society and the media on both sides. More important, closed-door dialogues made substantial progress in drafting the conditions for peace. In addition to confidence-building measures, including the resumption of a New Delhi-Lahore bus service, and a number of concessions on the Line of Control (LoC) in Kashmir, those back-channel negotiations launched in February 2004 brought India and Pakistan somewhat closer to agreement on Kashmir, the Siachen Glacier and Sir Creek, the key outstanding territorial issues.

But, true to the oscillatory nature of the India-Pakistan relationship, the progress of the Composite Dialogue was derailed after the 2008 Mumbai terrorist attacks. It was not until the "cricket diplomacy" between Pakistani Prime Minister Yousaf Raza Gillani and Indian Prime Minister Manmohan Singh at the March 2011 Cricket World Cup semifinal between India and Pakistan, that the two sides agreed to resume talks. (Stephanie Flamen-

However, just three months after Indian Prime Minister Vajpayee's symbolic ride on the inaugural bus trip from New Delhi to Lahore, the promises of that declaration were abandoned when military-backed Pakistani infiltrators triggered a limited war in the Kargil region of Kashmir. That infiltration was organized by Pakistan's then Chief of the Army Staff, Gen. Pervez Musharraf, who soon took over the reins of Pakistan in a military coup in 2000. Musharraf had kept Prime Minister Nawaz Sharif mostly in the dark while the latter was discussing resolving various issues with his Indian counterpart. (Nasim Zehra, *From Kargil to the Coup: Events that Shook Pakistan, 2018*)

Still, Vajpayee did not throw in the towel. In July 2001, he held a summit in Agra with Pakistan's then Chief Executive Pervez Musharraf, who had been instrumental in the Lahore Declaration's demise. Indian Prime Minister Vajpayee and Musharraf had one-on-one talks for more than eight hours during the two-day summit. The talks covered many bilateral issues, but concentrated on the Kashmir dispute. Pakistan insisted that Kashmir was the core issue, while India wanted a more broad-based dialogue including

CC/Nicholas (Nichalp)

Nariman House, a one of eight synagogues in Mumbai, after terrorists attacked on November 26, 2008.

baum and Megan Neville, *Optimism and Obstacles in India-Pakistan Peace Talks*, United States Institute of Peace, July 15, 2011)

Since the monstrous November 26-29, 2008 attacks in Mumbai, Pakistan-deployed terrorists have carried out a number of attacks on Indian security forces. One such notable attack took place on January 2, 2016, on a forward airbase near Pathankot, Punjab. This attack is significant because less than three weeks earlier, Indian Prime Minister Narendra Modi, on his way home from Kabul, had stopped in Pakistan. "Officials in Delhi and Islamabad told *The Hindu* that Mr. Modi had telephoned Prime Minister Nawaz Sharif from Kabul to greet him on his birthday, and during the call, made plans to travel to Lahore to wish him personally a few hours later." (Suhasini Haidar and Kallol Bhattacherjee, "PM Goes to Lahore, Makes a Christmas Date with History," *The Hindu,* Dec. 25, 2015) That was a major gesture, but Islamabad had no compunction in letting that one to go to waste, as well.

Despite those setbacks—and the sabotage organized by Pakistan's military, exploiting Pakistan's weak and fragile political system—there was no dearth of attempts to start talks between the two to ease tensions. A true peace, of course, was never on the horizon, since one party was aiding and abetting terrorist attacks against the other as the means to secure control over all of Jammu and Kashmir.

The Trust Issue

None of the peace efforts succeeded in easing tensions to the level at which serious discussions could take place. Perhaps the main ingredient missing was trust. Pakistan's governments, which fell under military domination soon after the country's inception, could never get past the knowledge that the breakup of the subcontinent was not acceptable to most Indians. This paranoia was spread throughout Pakistan by the military

archivepmo.nic.in

Indian Prime Minister Manmohan Singh with Pakistani Prime Minister Yousuf Raza Gilani in Mohali, March 30, 2011.

and later by the Islamic jihadis. It has been used to justify the Pakistan military's retention of the levers of power, and to argue that a democratic form of government under weak political elites would endanger the nation's existence. The Pakistani military has never stopped chanting this mantra.

As American academic Ashley Tellis noted in a 2017 paper for the U.S.-based think-tank, the Carnegie Endowment for International Peace, former Indian Prime Minister Atal Bihari Vajpayee had addressed this paranoia during his historic 1999 visit to Lahore. He used oratory and poetry to convey a significant message to the people of Pakistan when he visited their Minar-e-Pakistan national monument, boldly stating: "A stable, secure and prosperous Pakistan is in India's interest. Let no one in Pakistan be in doubt. India sincerely wishes Pakistan well." (Rakesh Sood, "To Talk or Not to Talk ...," *The Hindu,* Jan. 14, 2016)

Quoting Daniel S. Markey, a well-known American analyst of the subcontinent who stated, "most Indian

PIB of India

Indian Prime Minister Narendra Modi visits Pakistani Prime Minister Nawaz Sharif at Sharif's home in Raiwind. December 25, 2015.

strategists see Pakistan as a huge mess, not one India would want to inherit even if it had the military tools to sweep across the border unobstructed," Tellis sums up:

> India merely wants to be left alone: it desires that Islamabad and Rawalpindi [army headquarters] concentrate on their own domestic challenges and, recognizing the futility of pursuing an unattainable parity with New Delhi, permit India to advance its great-power ambitions in ways that will not undermine Pakistan's security, given its possession of nuclear weapons." (Ashley J. Tellis, *Are India-Pakistan Peace Talks Worth a Damn?* Carnegie Endowment for International Peace, 2017)

Some analysts are even blunter, arguing that, in fact, Pakistan has no legitimate claim at all against India. In a 2016 article, American academic C. Christine Fair, an associate professor at Georgetown University's Security Studies Program, succinctly summarizes why Pakistan continues to disregard peace with India as a necessity. Says Fair:

> Indians and the rest of the world must understand that the Pakistan army will always be a spoiler of even the most well-intended peace overture from Pakistan's beleaguered and besieged civilians. Once one realizes this, one must confront the very real question of the ultimate aim of this dialogue, because it cannot produce peace....
>
> In fact, there is no territorial dispute in which Pakistan has any defensible equities. Neither the Indian Independence Act of 1947 nor the Radcliffe Boundary Commission accord Pakistan any claim to Kashmir. The Indian Independence Act of 1947 averred that the sovereigns of princely states could choose which state to join. As is well-known, Maharaja of Kashmir Hari Singh only acceded to India after Pakistan dispatched irregular forces to seize the terrain by force. In fact, Pakistan makes this claim based

Pakistan Army troops on parade.

upon the Two Nation Theory, its communally bigoted founding ideology. (C. Christine Fair, "Denying Pakistan the Dividends of Terror," *Open* magazine, Sept. 23, 2016)

Changes in the Regional Environment

With that as background, conventional wisdom says that peace between India and Pakistan is well-nigh impossible. However, conventional wisdom has limitations grounded in time and environment. Global political situations, particularly in the region, have changed, although those changes have yet to be fully reflected in Pakistan's domestic political environment.

Changes in the region during the last few years have been extensive. Barring any unforeseeable event that may engulf the region in the coming years, these changes could bear healthy fruit. To begin with, the rise of China and India as major economic powers and their close relations with Russia, could make the Eurasian zone, along with Southeast and East Asia, the motor for development in the coming decades.

While India has done very well in maintaining, and even upgrading, its relations with these two areas of future prosperity, Pakistan has also made some progress. What makes India's success particularly laudable is that it has brought under its umbrella of economic partnership such important East Asian countries as Japan and South Korea, and to its west, almost all of the Gulf nations, including Iran. India's success with the Gulf countries and Iran—all Muslim nations—obliterates another piece of conventional wisdom, expressed mostly in the West—namely, that India is allergic to

Muslims.

There is, however, still one major caveat in the Eurasian zone (minus the Middle East)—and that is Afghanistan, a bordering neighbor of Pakistan, where hostilities continue with no solution in sight. This particular situation has also created a rush of bad blood between India and Pakistan, because the Pakistani military is actively involved in preventing any large-scale interaction between Afghanistan and India, contrary to the needs and the wishes of those two countries. Many Indian analysts and officials believe Washington is biased toward helping Pakistan—an old U.S. ally against the erstwhile Soviet Union—virtually ignoring all recent U.S. overtures toward India on Afghanistan. The late U.S. diplomat Richard Holbrooke's efforts in 2009 to include India in his Afghanistan-Pakistan portfolio were not only rejected by President Obama, but looked at suspiciously in New Delhi as well.

Among the environmental changes, topmost on the list is the growing prowess of Russia, India and China within the five-country BRICS organization—Brazil, Russia, India, China and South Africa. Although domestic problems within South Africa and Brazil have stymied the growth of the BRICS as a major economic powerhouse, the continuing growth of Russia, India and China has not slowed their economic and political interactions.

In addition to the BRICS, interaction between Russia, India and China has been given a boost in the Shanghai Cooperation Organization (SCO). The SCO was originally formed as the Shanghai Five—China, Russia, Kazakhstan, Kyrgyzstan and Tajikistan—in 1996. Following its inclusion of Uzbekistan as a full member in 2001, it was re-founded in Shanghai in 2001 and renamed the SCO. In 2017, India and Pakistan became full members. The SCO also has six dialogue partners, including Afghanistan and Iran.

After it was set up as a confidence-building forum to demilitarize borders, the organization's goals and agenda have since broadened to include increased military and counter-terrorism cooperation and intelligence sharing. The SCO has also intensified its focus on regional economic initiatives such as the recently announced integration of the China-led Silk Road Economic Belt and the Russia-led Eurasian Economic Union.

Sahiwal coal-fired power plant in Pakistan's Punjab province, the first major energy project of the China-Pakistan Economic Corridor, inaugurated July 3, 2017.

The potential for the SCO to be effective is manifold. By including Pakistan as a full member, and having Afghanistan as an observer, the "Big Three"—Russia, China and India—have created an opportunity to deal with terrorism and drug-trafficking issues which, if not handled with firm determination, could affect the developmental plans of the "Big Three" and weaken their ability to play a global role.

Terrorism already affects all three directly. In India, the terrorism instigated and orchestrated from Rawalpindi and Islamabad in the Indian part of Jammu and Kashmir continues, despite various measures undertaken by New Delhi. In addition, heroin/opium moving in from Afghanistan through Pakistan in the west, has bolstered the financing of the terrorists in the state of Jammu and Kashmir, and unleashed a drug epidemic in the Indian state of Punjab.

In Russia, particularly in the northern Caucasus, Islamic jihadis have established their presence over the decades. Among the most affected areas are Chechnya, Dagestan, Ingushetia and North Ossetia; but the terrorists have reared their heads in Tatarstan as well.

Work Cut Out for China

For China, a terrorist-free Eurasian zone is the key to making its visionary Silk Road Economic Belt (henceforth identified as the Belt and Road Initiative, or BRI program), viable and beneficial for the host and recipient countries. The BRI runs through the Central Asian countries to Russia and Europe, and also to the Gulf countries through Iran. China has invested heavily in this enterprise to make these transport corridors a success. However, if China does not step up to the plate in dealing with the drug traffickers and terrorists who roam virtually free in these sparsely populated areas, Beijing's dream of interlinking China through roads and railways with Central Asia, Europe and the Middle East could end up in tatters.

China has also invested heavily in Pakistan, where terrorists, some of whom operate under the protective umbrella of the Pakistani Inter-Services Intelligence (ISI), remain active. China is planning to invest some $60 billion in Pakistan to upgrade roads and railways, to build a port in Gwadar City on the Arabian Sea close to the Iranian border, and to build hydro- and coal-based power plants. This scheme, which is very much underway now, is known as the China-Pakistan Economic Corridor (CPEC), and one of its arteries passes through secessionist and terrorist-infested Balochistan Province to Gwadar—a key destination of China. The BRI is not a one-shot deal—its utility will be realized on the basis of its 24/7 operations spread over the coming years. That means that the entire area around these installations has to remain terrorist-free and stable.

Another Positive Development

Another noticeable change in the area that could help start a real peace process between India and Pakistan, is what could be described as the apparent "rapprochement" between Russia and Pakistan. During the Cold War, Moscow considered Islamabad a facilitator of its adversary (for good reason). Pakistan had surreptitiously provided the United States a base in Peshawar to carry out surveillance on the Soviet Union. That was exposed in the 1960 U-2 spy plane incident. Then, following the Red Army's invasion of Afghanistan in 1979, and throughout its decade-long stay in that country, Pakistan was a conduit for the West and Saudi Arabia to recruit, train and arm Islamic jihadis brought in from Arabia and beyond, to fight and kill Russian military personnel.

Although the Soviet Union ceased to exist in 1991, the bad blood between Moscow and Islamabad continued to flow for almost another three decades. But today that seems to have changed. Lately, Russia has extended a friendly hand toward Pakistan. Since 2015, the chiefs of Pakistan's Army, Navy and Air Force have traveled to Russia. The flurry of high-level exchanges

mil.ru

Serviceman of Russia and Pakistan storm a base as part of their joint military exercise Friendship-2016. Cherat range, Pakistan.

between the two nations resulted in the signing of a deal for the sale of four Mi-35 attack helicopters to Islamabad. In September 2016, about 200 troops from the two countries were involved in a two-week military drill named "Friendship 2016." A Russian ground forces contingent came to Pakistan to participate in the first-ever joint military exercises. ("Russian Troops Arrive in Pakistan for First-Ever Joint Drills," PTI, Sept. 23, 2016)

Equally significant is the recent visit to Russia of Pakistan's Vice Chief of the Naval Staff, Vice Admiral Kaleem Shaukat. Just now, on July 31, Shaukat met Commander-in-Chief of the Russian Federation Navy, Admiral Vladimir Ivanovich Korolyov, at the Central Naval Museum in St. Petersburg. They discussed professional matters, bilateral naval collaboration, and the security environment in the Indian Ocean region. Admiral Shaukat also attended the main naval parade on the occasion of Russian Federation Navy Day, besides visiting a naval shipyard and the frigate *Admiral Makarov.* ("Pakistan, Russia Sign MoU for Naval Cooperation," *The Nation,* July 31, 2018)

If the Russia-Pakistan "rapprochement," which is still in an early stage, does, indeed, materialize, it would help India. It would mean that Russia, a well-wisher of India, alongside China, can bring full-court pressure on Pakistan to stop aiding the anti-India terrorists, and act as a responsible nation by accepting the basic principles on which an India-Pakistan peace process could begin.

Tell-Tale Signs

There is no guarantee that the changes mentioned above will automatically create the environment for starting a peace process. On the ground, there is no such indication yet. Only recently, Pakistan refused to adhere to the 2003 ceasefire understanding to not use its violations at the LoC to provide cover for infiltration. The Indian government says that in 2018 alone, there have already been more than 1,000 violations of the 2003 ceasefire agreement between New Delhi and Islamabad, by the Pakistani side. ("India Asks Pakistan to Adhere to 2003 Ceasefire Agreement," TNN, Jun. 8, 2018)

These violations are clear indications that the Pakistani military wants to continue its anti-India jihad, throwing caution to the wind. On the other hand, some of the recent statements by top Pakistani military officials indicate a subtle shift in tone. In April, Pakistan's Chief of Army Staff, General Qamar Javed Bajwa, invited Sanjay Vishwasrao, the Indian military attaché, and his team to the Pakistan Day military parade in Islamabad. The Royal United Services Institute (RUSI, a British defense and security think tank, whose director is Karin von Hippel, former chief of staff to U.S. General John Allen, special presidential envoy for the Global Coalition to Counter-ISIL) described the gesture as "historic," noting:

> And, in a sign that ties between the two foes are warming up, Javed Bajwa followed this two weeks later by saying that the Pakistan military wanted peace and dialogue with India. (Kamal Alam, "Pakistan's Military Reaches Out to India," RUSI, May 3, 2018)

As RUSI also pointed out,

> Bajwa himself, speaking at RUSI last year, announced that "the Pakistan army is now no more insecure and feels confident of its future," and that he welcomes Indian participation in Pakistan's flagship infrastructure project, the China Pakistan Economic Corridor.

Another statement issued recently by Pakistan's military spokesman is also significant. Speaking at a press briefing on June 4, military spokesperson Major-General Asif Ghafoor said he wished for all issues between the nuclear-armed neighbors to be resolved through dialogue. "War is a failure of diplomacy," Ghafoor said. "We are two nuclear states; there is no space for war. So dialogue continues. India has always been the one to back out from dialogue, not Pakistan." (Asad Hashim, "Pakistani Military Says 'No Space for War' with India," PTI, June 4, 2018)

Do these statements imply that the paranoia, the policy of bleeding India, and the siege mentality that have driven Rawalpindi's policies for decades have begun to wane? It would be naive to assume that that has happened.

Some wonder if the arrival of Imran Khan as the new leader of Pakistan's weak political system will help the peace process. Imran Khan has very little experience in dealing with international and domestic security, and economic and political affairs. Moreover, he will have to preside over an economy that is badly in debt, and a currency that is falling rapidly. Until such time as he emerges as a leader who is in control of the Pakistani political minefield set up by veteran Punjabi and Sindhi politicians, while still able to retain Rawalpindi's confidence, that question cannot be answered.

Conclusion

In concluding, a note on border disputes of the kind that exist between India and Pakistan, is in order. These border disputes should not be allowed to perpetuate animosity and hostility. Look, for example, at Sino-Indian relations. India and China have a longstanding, fundamental dispute over their borders. Both sides understand that these border disputes will not be settled in the near term. Yet Sino-Indian relations are developing in many other directions. Economic interactions, as well as bilateral trade and promises of cooperation in security matters, are growing.

Finally, it is also important to note that the mere cessation of hostilities, or simply ceasing fire along the borders, are not the entire definition of "peace." While cessation of hostilities is the necessary first step, what makes "peace" worthwhile, is developing interaction between the two countries at every level—ensuring security, strengthening economic relations, engaging in joint innovative projects, setting up transport corridors, and enhancing bilateral trade.

To make India-Pakistan peace worthwhile, both sides need to embrace the whole process.

New Paradigm Moves Forward with 'Singapore Model': Dialogue, Not War!

This is the edited transcript of the August 2, 2018 Schiller Institute New Paradigm webcast, an interview with the founder of the Schiller Institutes, Helga Zepp-LaRouche. She was interviewed by Harley Schlanger. A video of the webcast is available.

Harley Schlanger: Hello, I'm Harley Schlanger with the Schiller Institute. Welcome to this week's international strategic webcast with Helga Zepp-La-Rouche, who is the founder of the Schiller Institutes, and who is at the forefront of the fight for bringing together a New Paradigm, to replace the collapsing, dangerous old paradigm of geopolitical confrontation.

Following the BRICS Summit featuring the leaders of the BRICS nations—Brazil, Russia, India, China and South Africa—last week's developments have further consolidated that New Paradigm—a series of new initiatives, dialogues opening, and dialogues continuing. There were hysterical counter-reactions coming from the City of London and the neo-cons in the United States.

Helga, why don't we start with the continuing momentum from the BRICS Summit in Johannesburg, because there's a lot to report. Why don't you give us an update on what you know about that?

Post-Summit New Paradigm Progress

Helga Zepp-LaRouche: Yes, we discussed this last week, but since then, more reports have revealed that, in addition to the BRICS Summit itself, the BRICS Plus and BRICS Outreach programs brought in representatives of very many of all important developing-country organizations, such as the G-77, Mercosur, the Organization of Islamic Cooperation, and many regional organizations. One can say that what is emerging is very, very rapidly becoming a completely new economic order, a new system of governance based on win-win cooperation and full respect for the sovereignty of each nation. This is really delivering on the New Silk Road Spirit, which has now captured the majority of nations, at least of the Southern Hemisphere and the developing sector.

This is creating completely different conditions for those nations involved, so that many conflicts which had seemed unresolvable, are now being worked out in a peaceful manner. I'll give you just one example: Pakistan's new Prime Minister, Imran Khan, has now said that Pakistan will follow the Chinese model; he also said that he wants rapprochement with India. For every positive step India makes in respect to Pakistan, he is willing to take two steps. So there is actually, for the first time,

The leaders of the BRICS (front row) and their Outreach guests at the annual BRICS Summit, Johannesburg, South Africa, July 25-27, 2018.

the possibility of resolving the India-Pakistan conflict. For the first time, Russia's and Pakistan's militaries have conducted joint maneuvers.

China plays a big role in Pakistan. Russia has very good relations with India. And now the new spirit of the enlarged Shanghai Cooperation Organization makes it more possible to resolve this conflict.

The North Korea breakthrough in Singapore, which we discussed in previous webcasts, contrary to the media lies, is on a very good track—it's moving forward in the right way. The New Silk Road Spirit has caught on in the Horn of Africa. For the first time we are witnessing a rapprochement among the nations of Somalia, Djibouti, Eritrea, and Ethiopia.

In this context, the Houthi leader in Yemen made a unilateral peace offer to the other side: saying that for the sake of the peace of the Yemeni people who are suffering the worst humanitarian catastrophe on the planet, there should be a ceasefire and a move towards peace.

I think all of these developments are really absolutely fantastic, and they show that under the leadership of the BRICS nations—China, Russia, India, South Africa and Brazil—there is an effort to replace the old, collapsed, geopolitical order with a new system of international relationships, which I think is very, very promising. It's horrible that our mainstream media in the West are so *gleichgeschaltet*, so absolutely controlled, that most people know absolutely nothing about these fantastic developments, because the media just don't report it. But that doesn't mean it doesn't exist.

So therefore, I appeal to you, our viewers, to make sure that this program becomes more known—share among your friends and acquaintances, and join the Schiller Institute. We have to get the West to participate in shaping the new world economic order. It's absolutely possible, it can be done; however, there is a lot of work to be done to bring Europe and the United States into this new paradigm of global relations centered on real economic development for everyone on the planet.

Peace Breaks Out in Syria

Schlanger: It's somewhat unbelivable, the degree to which these developments are not reported. One example that you've brought up, and that the Schiller In-

Imran Khan, Pakistan's new Prime Minister.

stitute has been very much involved in promoting, is the effort to reconstruct the Syrian city of Aleppo, which was destroyed largely because of Western support—British, American, Obama support—for the terrorists inside Syria. And now there's motion to reconstruct that city. This is part of the New Paradigm, isn't it?

Zepp-LaRouche: Yes. You would think that the Western media and politicians, especially in Europe which has been completely destabilized and shaken up by the refugee crisis, would be among the first to report this, but, no, they don't. The Governor of Aleppo has announced a three-part program: first, to rebuild the infrastructure; second to help every single affected family; and third, to bring them safely back into the reconstructed Aleppo. There is also a Russian refugee center in Syria, where refugees returning from Jordan, Lebanon, and Turkey are being brought back to their respective regions.

You would think that this would be capturing the news headlines: that the refugee crisis can now be solved by rebuilding the country. It's completely outrageous that the knowledge of these developments is being kept from the citizens of the United States and most European nations. I must say: The story about who created and who finances the White Helmets, and who invented the false narrative against Syria, must come out, and indeed, will come out, and the criminals responsible will be brought to justice.

A New Role for Italy ...

Schlanger: Another very important example of non-coverage was the July 30 meeting at the White House between President Trump and Italian Prime Minister Giuseppe Conte. The European and American media gave big play to the fight between Trump and the Europeans at the recent NATO Summit. There has been a constant media barrage against the Italians in the European media. With the Trump-Conte meeting, which seemed to have quite a bit of substance, there is virtually no coverage in those same media outlets.

Are people in Europe aware of the importance of this meeting, and is this getting around to the people you're talking to, Helga?

Zepp-LaRouche: There has been some reporting of the meeting, which was really historic. Trump and Conte formed a new strategic partnership between the United States and Italy, especially to address the crisis in Libya, but also, Trump said he recognizes the Italian leadership role for the entire Mediterranean. I think this is very good. They struck up an immediate friendship. Naturally, the German media were quite freaked out, and they talked about a "new axis" between Washington and Rome, against the Berlin-Paris "axis." This is all quite ridiculous, but it is one more instance showing that the famous European unity does not exist, and will not exist because the policies of the EU are such that they make enemies out of their own members. So, this Conte-Trump development is very positive.

White House/D. Myles Cullen

President Trump (right) in bilateral meeting with Italian Prime Minister Conte at the White House, Washington, D.C., July 30, 2018.

Schlanger: Part of that is that the new government coming into power in Italy, was not only opposed by the EU bureaucracy, but one of the reasons it was opposed is its support for Glass-Steagall—among some in the Lega party in the coalition government. I bring this up because there's a huge fight emerging in Europe over what's going to happen to the City of London in Brexit. We have the derivatives crisis, with the City of London threatening Europe that it will not provide backup for derivatives. This is set to explode, isn't it?

Zepp-LaRouche: Yes, there is very clear panic. The British financial "industry" is about the only "industry" they have. The demand now is, according to unnamed British government officials, that despite the Brexit, that unless City of London firms are allowed free rein to sell derivatives contracts in the

EU, EU firms will be excluded from the UK, that is, that the City keeps control over European derivatives trading. Now, this unnamed government official said, if this not allowed, then thousands of investment firms will go bankrupt, and that this is not a threat, he says, but a warning of how much both sides could lose if a deal is not struck in Britain's favor.

Now, this is really mafia talk. The fact that Deutsche Bank moved its derivatives trading to Frankfurt, was commented on by multibillionaire Sir Alan Sugar—not so sweet, but that's his name—who said that the fact that Deutsche Bank moved its derivatives trading to Frankfurt is the beginning of the end of the importance of London as a financial headquarters of the world. Jamie Dimon, Chairman and CEO of JPMorgan Chase, has also warned that the quantitative easing must continue, or else financial panic could break out.

Despite the fact that in some places, people pretend it doesn't exist, the danger of a new financial blowout is imminent all the time and could be triggered by anything. We need to have Glass-Steagall in place.

When Prime Minister Conte arrived at the White House, he saw the big banner our colleagues in the United States had made: "Benvenuto Prime Minister Conte. Go for Glass-Steagall!" He waved in recognition. This was all covered very nicely by some Italian media, quite surprised to find such a warm welcome for their prime minister.

This is all very interesting. It really makes clear how super-urgent it is to enact the Four Laws of Lyndon LaRouche. Glass-Steagall, a national bank, a credit system, and a New Bretton Woods are all absolutely urgent.

The only country seriously doing anything about that financial crisis is China. There were meetings recently led by President Xi Jinping and State Council Premier Li Keqiang, including practically the entire Chinese leadership, warning of potential external shocks and the completely changing international environment—therefore China needs to focus on the physical economy, strengthen small and micro-firms, strengthen R&D and innovation. All kinds of speculation must be curbed to secure the country against external shocks.

So I can only say it would be good if the Western governments would all learn from this Chinese approach. If you have an uncontrolled collapse, we will be in a terrible chaos in no time.

… and Mexico and North Korea

Schlanger: It's somewhat ironic that Jamie Dimon and people of his ilk are saying that the solution is more funny money from the central banks! Whereas the Chinese are saying, "more production, more investment." And that, of course, is the message that you and your husband have been fighting for, for years.

I want to bring up another example of what we were talking about earlier: the kind of potential that exists within the New Paradigm. One that's very shocking to most people, is the potential for an emerging relationship between President Trump and López Obrador, the President-elect of Mexico. Kesha Rogers, a LaRouche

PAC-endorsed candidate for Congress from Texas's 9th CD, issued a proposal for a North American Belt and Road Initiative (NABRI). What you do think about that, Helga?

Zepp-LaRouche: I think it is a brilliant idea, because there was discussion from President Trump to renegotiate NAFTA. But why would you renegotiate something which was so absolutely detrimental to the interests of every participating country: Canada, the United States, and Mexico? And therefore, she proposed not NAFTA, but NABRI, picking up on President-elect López Obrador's invitation to the United States to invest in infrastructure projects in Mexico, as the best way to solve the migrant problem.

This is very good, and Rogers told me that she is planning a whole bunch of events around that, both in the United States and also involving Mexico. The Schiller Institute has been campaigning for the United States and European countries, but especially the United States, to join with the Belt and Road Initiative and make joint investments in South and Central America for infrastructure projects, in the tradition of what my husband had worked out with Mexican President José López Portillo more than 35 years ago, in *Operation Juárez*, for an integrated infrastructure plan for all of Latin America.

All that is now absolutely back on the table. China is having many dealings with the Latin American countries. And it's very good that López Obrador invited both Xi and Trump to his December 1 inauguration. I think there is great recognition that there is no contradiction in the United States and China working together with the Latin American countries to bring them out of poverty, to bring them into a better way of life. I think that is the way to go. I think you will hear a lot from Rogers about this in the next month.

Schlanger: It might be appropriate to make sure that Trump, Xi, and López Obrador have copies of your husband's *Operation Juárez* pamphlet, because that actually shaped the fight that was going on in the 1980s—

the debt bomb and the move away from a bankrupt system. Instead, the West doubled down on speculation, deregulation and so on, and wrecked everything.

Giving Up the Failed Geopolitics

Zepp-LaRouche: They just can't get rid of their old, geopolitical thinking. One good example of that thinking is former Secretary of State Henry Kissinger who, according to some press accounts has advised Trump to work with Russia to contain the rise of China. You know, it's funny, because in 1971, when I was in China for the first time, the news was announced that Kissinger would come and visit China. If I remember correctly, he was then advising the Chinese against Russia. So these people just cannot think in terms of the higher idea of one mankind, "a community of a shared future of humanity," as Xi always calls it. They can only think in terms of a zero-sum game; they can only think one must lose so the other can win.

In spite of the likes of Henry Kissinger, a New Paradigm *is* coming into being very, very quickly, and it is win-win! Everybody wins, if you respect the interest of the other and vice versa. I think this new world economic order is marching in *very* quickly. Almost every day you have a breathtaking, positive development. The only problem is, if we don't manage to get the West—the United States and the European nations—on board, they will be sidelined. They will be completely unimportant, to the detriment of their own populations. That is the only thing we should be worried about, so we must increase our efforts to get them to join the New Paradigm.

Schlanger: There was also a new exchange between President Trump and Kim Jong-un of North Korea, an exchange of letters: Trump thanked Kim for returning the remains of 55 U.S. soldiers from the Korean War and referred to the possibility of Kim addressing the United Nations General Assembly in September. Again, this is something which should have received headline coverage, and more importantly, it should have received an enthusiastic response from all political quarters. But again, we have seen a reaction against that. How do you see things shaping up between the United States and North Korea? There's a lot of continuing back-biting and nasty coverage in the media;

U.S. Vice President Mike Pence participates in the honorable carry ceremony for U.S. soldiers killed in the Korean War. Joint Base Pearl Harbor-Hickam, Honolulu, Hawaii, Aug. 1, 2018.

but it does appear as though there's some progress.

Zepp-LaRouche: Yes. Kim Jong-un sent a letter to Trump, writing that he's convinced that epochal changes will come out of their next meeting, which he is looking forward to. Kim mentioned Trump's tweet in which Trump thanked Kim for releasing the remains of the U.S. soldiers. All the signs point to progress that is continuously moving forward. The fake news media is just at it again.

Declassify Remaining 9/11 Documents

Schlanger: Helga, something came up that I think the Schiller Institute would very much support: a call to release all 9/11 documents. An enormous amount remains classified. Do you think releasing those documents would have a powerful effect?

Zepp-LaRouche: Oh, absolutely. The 9/11 story was a game-changer for the United States and in different ways for the rest of the world. Rep. Walter Jones in the House and Sen. Richard Blumenthal in the Senate, have both said they plan to introduce resolutions calling for declassifying all remaining documents related to the victims of the Sept. 11, 2001 terrorist attacks. And I think Blumenthal said: Look, put yourself in this position: Assume you were a family member of one of the victims and you are looking at the documents and then you come to the part where it says, "and the following persons are guilty for this," and then it's blacked out, blacked out, blacked out. He said that these family members have the absolute right to know who is responsible for the deaths of their loved ones.

Quite interesting in this context, is that an FBI agent, who was the one who warned in July 2001 that there were plans by Saudi Arabia for a terrorist attack in the United States—which was not followed up at the time—said that he was told to do everything in his power to prevent the 9/11 families from suing Saudi Arabia. He has now said that he feels it's his duty to speak out on this.

In addition, Congressman Devin Nunes has demanded that all the documents related to the FISA warrant regarding the Christopher Steele dossier and the whole coup against Trump be declassified. Nunes said if the American people were to read these documents, they would be shocked. He promised that, despite the Congressional recess, his committee would stay through August and work overtime, to have interviews, to have people subpoenaed, investigate them, and absolutely stay at it.

We have not seen the end of it. Trump suggested in a tweet, two or three days ago, that Attorney General Jeff Sessions should just shut down this witch hunt given that Special Counsel Robert Mueller has so many conflicts of interest; it should just be shut down. This could actually happen; perhaps criminal prosecution of the guilty parties would follow soon after.

We do need to support the demand that the 9/11 documents be declassified. This is one of the three areas that point to the role of Robert Mueller—not the only case, but one of them—and therefore, it is extremely important. If the United States is to go back to being a full constitutional republic, then the damage of the Bush-Cheney-British use of the 9/11 attacks, and everything which came with it, must be reversed.

Schlanger: It's not surprising that Mueller was trying to use classification and other means to suppress the emergence of these documents. I saw a one-minute clip on YouTube of Mueller testifying before Congress in the time after the 9/11 attacks, fully endorsing the war against Iraq, saying that there was definite evidence that Saddam Hussein had weapons of mass destruction.

He was clearly part of developing the narrative that led to the war. The anger against that false narrative played a very significant role in Trump's election victory— Trump attacked George W. Bush for lying to the American people over this.

Another story that has to come out is real nature of the situation in Ukraine. Sergey Lavrov, the Russian Foreign Minister, has been in some discussions recently on the real facts on the ground in Ukraine: It is the government of Ukraine, the Kiev regime, that is blocking any progress. Helga, is there any chance that this is going to come to fruition, or is this going to continue to be a sticking point in improvement of Western relations with Russia?

The Ukraine-EU Nightmare, and Africa's Dreams

Zepp-LaRouche: Lavrov actually said that behind closed doors, many Western leaders will admit that they are quite aware that Kiev is controlled by Nazis, but these same leaders don't have the courage to say so publicly. This is an ongoing problem. Not only did the Obama Administration—Victoria Nuland and her friends in the EU—back the coup in Ukraine, but this group is now doing exactly the same sort of operation— or trying to—this time in Zimbabwe. Zimbabwe just had an election in which the ruling party was re-elected, winning an overwhelming majority of seats in Parliament.

Elmar Brok, a German member of the European Parliament, who is associated with the Bertelsmann Foundation, was the only election observer, among all the observers there from many different organizations, who claimed election irregularities. This is the same

Brok who played a leading role in the Maidan fascist coup in Ukraine—cheering and steering demonstrators to bring down the elected government. In Zimbabwe, he demanded that the election results be published immediately, even though it normally takes five days until all the results are known. Brok demanded this, saying there was great mistrust of the election authorities. His accusations were then the trigger for the Movement for Democratic Change to call for riots.

People started to burn cars and other property. In the context of this violence, three people were killed and many wounded. There is video footage of these things, so we can expect that there will be some follow-up. Inciting people to violence, violence in which people are killed, is a serious crime. An appropriate response should be expected.

This illustrates that elements within the EU are not only blocking the collaboration of Africa and other regions with China, but are continuing the policy of regime change and destabilization. This should be denounced and must be stopped.

Schlanger: Helga, we've covered a lot. Is there anything we've missed that you want to bring up?

Zepp-LaRouche: Let's go back to where we started this discussion. There is so much reason for hope. With peace processes involving India, Pakistan, the Koreas, the Horn of Africa, and an absolute commitment to overcoming underdevelopment and poverty in the developing countries, we have reason for great joy. The reality is that there is a bright future now unfolding—despite the hysteria being created on many fronts by various forces in the West. Germany is a sad example, using this heat wave that is causing terrible damage to the farmers and creating other problems, to go completely overboard, saying we now need to completely abandon the use of coal to reduce CO_2 in the atmosphere. There is even a call for a commission on vehicular traffic to discuss how to reduce traffic.

EU observers red flag Zim vote; cite misuse of state resources, media bias

Elmar Brok, German European Parliament Member. He was the only Zimbabwe election observer to claim election irregularities.

All of Africa will soon have nuclear plants, and they're perfectly manageable. At the BRICS Summit, Russian President Vladimir Putin said that Russia will help to "light up Africa" by installing electrical generating capacity, powered by not only gas and oil, but especially nuclear energy—a field in which Russia is the world's technological leader—for the 600 million people in Africa who still don't have electricity. Many other developing countries are going in the same direction of building nuclear plants, which are absolutely manageable by humanity.

And if countries such as Germany remain in their super-greenie fit, it is terrible, and they will collapse! Since I love my country—I'm not only a world citizen, but I'm also a patriot—I really think we have to change our ways and go back to the humanist values we used to have in Germany, when we thought of Germany as a country of poets, thinkers and inventors. I'm not giving up hope, but we need a change. I have always said that it is probable that Germany will be the last country to come around, but if it's surrounded by countries all wanting to be part of the Belt and Road, which is increasingly happening in Europe, eventually we'll crack even Germany.

So, I'm optimistic. It's a challenging situation, the world is extremely complex, but the vector of development is positive. So, join the Schiller Institute and help us continue this work until we have brought the world into safe waters.

Schlanger: If people want to share Helga's optimism, you need to not only catch the New Silk Road Spirit, but spread it. Make sure to tune in every week to this webcast. Help us build the audience and build the membership of the Schiller Institute. And Helga, sitting here in Germany with you in this heat wave, I can attest to the fact that we need more nuclear plants in Germany, so we can have some more air conditioning here.

So until next week, thanks again, Helga.

Ethiopia Targeted for Destabilization

by Dean Andromidas

Aug. 6—On July 26, on the day Ethiopian Prime Minister Abiy Ahmed left on his first official trip to Washington, D.C., Simegnew Bekele, the chief engineer of the Grand Ethiopian Renaissance Dam—one of the country's most important Chinese-backed infrastructure projects—was assassinated. His body was found in his Toyota 4X4 in Meskel Square, the nerve center of Addis Abeba, with a gunshot wound in his head. Simegnew had become a legendary figure in Ethiopia for his championing and managing not only of the Renaissance Dam project, but several others that have significantly increased the country's power generation capacity. Addressing a gathering of the Ethiopian North American Muslim Foundation (BADR), in Virginia, Prime Minister Abiy stated: "The circumstances of his death—in daylight at the heart of our capital—are a provocation to shake our resolve." He vowed that justice will be served.

The murder was a brutal show of force by powerful international interests determined to stop Ethiopia and all of Africa in their fight for rapid economic and industrial development by cooperating with China's Belt and Road Initiative. Simegnew's murder was preceded by an assassination attempt against Ethiopian Prime Minister Abiy on June 23 at a massive rally at the same location, in support of his reform policy (See "Ethiopia: Dramatic Policy Shift Puts Regional Development at Center Stage," *EIR*, Volume 45, Number 30, July 27, 2018).

Simegnew was the leading engineer and architect of Ethiopia's vision of creating an extensive network of large hydroelectric projects with the goal of making huge leaps in the country's electricity generating capacity. When the reservoir of the $4 billion (3.2 billion euro) Renaissance Dam is full, the hydroelectric dam will

ethembe.se

Engineer Simegnew Bekele, Project Manager of the Grand Ethiopian Renaissance Dam.

Juergen Ponto

Hanns Martin Schleyer

Alfred Herrhausen

Detlev Rohwedder

have the largest capacity in Africa, capable of producing more than 6,000 megawatts of electricity, providing a 50% increase in the country's installed capacity. It was financed in part by China. The Italian engineering firm Salini-Impregilo was the contractor. Electricity generated by the dam's turbines will power the expanding national railway network. The first stretch of that rail grid, which connects Addis Abeba to the Port of Djibouti, was built in collaboration with China.

The assassination of engineers and scientists—symbols of Africa's commitment to building mega-infrastructure projects with the intention of leapfrogging the continent into the industrial world—should be taken seriously by all the countries on the continent.

Founder of the Schiller Institutes, Helga Zepp-LaRouche, has compared this assassination to those that took place in Germany in the 1970s and 1980s, which targeted scientists, business leaders, and financiers who were key figures in the growth and spread of Germany's nuclear industry, and who favored providing this technology to the developing sector. A short review of those targeted will confirm the parallel.

• In July 1977, the terrorist Baader-Meinhof gang, later known as the Red Army Faction (RAF), assassinated Juergen Ponto, director of Dresdner Bank. Just before his death, in an interview in the South African magazine, *To the Point International*, he called for the dismantling of racial discrimination in South Africa. He called for Germany and the other leading nations of Europe to cooperate with the nations of Africa in the economic development of the continent. He also called for the development of nuclear power in Africa, as well as a reform of the European financial systems to facilitate the extension of credit for development projects.

• The following September, Ponto's murder was followed by the kidnapping and murder of Hanns Martin Schleyer, Chairman of the German Employers Association.

• By the 1980s the same terrorist group was targeting scientists and engineers, paralleling the dismantling of Germany's sophisticated nuclear power industry. In February 1985, the RAF assassinated Dr. Ernst Zimmermann, Chairman of the Federal Association of German Aerospace Industries. He was also the head of the MTU of Germany, a leading aerospace company.

• In July 1986, the RAF assassinated Prof. Karl Heinz Beckurts, the head of Research and Technology for Siemens. He also headed the German Atomic Forum. Beckurts played a leading role in developing Germany's nuclear industry. He also assisted Brazil in developing its nuclear sector.

• Alfred Herrhausen, Chairman of Deutsche Bank, Germany's largest bank, was assassinated in 1989. His armored car was targeted by a remotely triggered roadside bomb. The assassination was attributed to the unheard of "Second generation RAF." No one was ever arrested, nor has any member of this phantom group ever been identified. Herrhausen was a key adviser to then Chancellor Helmut Kohl on important economic policy issues related to the economic collapse of East Germany and Eastern Europe after the disintegration of the Soviet

Ethiopian Prime Minister Abiy Ahmed.

Union. He was also about to depart for New York City to deliver a speech to the Council on Foreign Relations. In segments of the speech which have been published, he intended to call for a debt moratorium for developing countries.

• In April 1991, Detlev Rohwedder was assassinated by a sniper. He headed the Treuhand, the German state organization responsible for selling or rehabilitating East German industrial enterprises. He was a key figure in the government's economic planning after reunification. This assassination was also attributed to terrorists. No arrest has ever been made in this crime.

These assassinations put an end to Germany's leadership role in the nuclear power and aerospace sectors, and served to lock Germany into the grip of the "Brussels consensus" of the European Union, which had policies targeting Russia and China, while maintaining a Malthusian policy towards Africa.

Simegnew's assassination must be taken as a warning to all of Africa, and appropriate security measures must be taken. As for Ethiopia, his assassination is not likely to weaken the resolve of the political leadership. The ruling Ethiopian Peoples' Revolutionary Democratic Front (EPRDF) has its roots in a liberation struggle of the 1970s and 1980s against a foreign-backed and brutal military dictatorship. The EPRDF has a powerful

President of Somalia Mohammed Abdullahi Mohamed (Farmajo).

vision for Ethiopia to become a strong industrial nation. Ethiopia has chosen key aspects of the "China model" with its emphasis on building national infrastructure. This has already earned the country the reputation of being the "China of Africa."

Neither the assassination attempt against Abiy nor the murder of Simegnew has stopped the forward momentum of the new government's reform policy that calls for peace and economic development in domestic and foreign policy.

On the day of Simegnew's assassination, Aiby was already in the United States on an unofficial visit to meet with the Ethiopian diaspora, including leaders of the opposition Gunbot 7, in his effort to promote reconciliation and unity among all sectors of Ethiopian society. His message included a call for the diaspora to contribute to the development of their homeland, including returning to participate in the hard work ahead. He especially took this message to the highly educated young professionals, including medical doctors, scientists, and engineers, whose knowledge and skills are needed back home.

Expanding the Circle of Peace and Development

As referenced in the *EIR* article cited above, all this occurs in a historic moment for Ethiopia, which has just re-established relations with Eritrea, twenty years after its bloody war of secession. Full diplomatic relations between the two countries were established during the visit of Eritrean President Isaias Afwerki to Ethiopia on July 14. Now, ambitious plans for economic integration have been discussed, including reconstruction of the highway between Ethiopia and the two Red Sea ports in Eritrea.

As a result of Abiy's region-wide initiative, the Eritrean President has has moved to expand the circle of peace and development the two leaders initiated, to the rest of the war-torn Horn of Africa. Afwerki invited the President of Somalia, Mohammed Abdullahi "Farmajo" to Eritrea. Mohammed made an official visit to Eritrea on July

28, the first for a Somali President. Prior to his invitation, Eritrea and Somalia had had very strained relations, because some of the armed anti-government opposition in Somalia was being supplied via Eritrea.

Speaking at a banquet in honor of the Somali President, Afwerki praised all three countries for overcoming the forms of subversion, including by the "misguided policies of powerful countries," that have thrown the region into a quarter-century of chaos and suffering. Afwerki stated:

CC/Reinhard Dietrich
Port Massawa on the Red Sea coast of Eritrea, Jan. 10, 2011.

> But this epoch of crises, conflict, and instability is not inherently sustainable. As such, it is nearing its end. We are indeed entering a new, transitional, phase.
>
> The people of Eritrea have demonstrated exceptional resilience to challenge and frustrate all forms of subversion directed at them. They have prevailed in spite of the transgressions and pressures to which they were subjected without let-up. The people of Ethiopia have triumphed over the politics of ethnic polarization and foreign subservience. They are marching forward at a rapid pace for the crystallization and consolidation of a correct national and regional policy framework. There is no doubt whatsoever that the people of Somalia will, as ever, be fellow travelers with the peoples of Ethiopia and Eritrea.

The Somali President was accompanied by his ministers of Information, Culture and Tourism, Transportation, and Construction, as well as the State Minister in the Ministry of Foreign Affairs. Wide ranging discussions were held on the development of bilateral relations. The presidents toured development projects in Eritrea. They signed a joint communiqué pledging to "forge intimate political, economic, social, cultural, as well as defense and security cooperation." They agreed to "establish diplomatic relations and exchange ambassadors, promote bilateral trade and investment, as well as educational and cultural exchanges." They pledged to "work in unison to foster regional peace, stability and economic integration."

Earlier this month, President Mohammed Abdullahi hosted Ethiopian Prime Minister Abiy Ahmed. The two leaders signed accords for far-reaching economic cooperation. The two leaders also attended the opening of the first phase of the Djibouti International Free Trade Zone, which was established in cooperation with China.

The border dispute between Eritrea and Djibouti still has to be resolved to normalize relations between those two countries. Ethiopia has offered to mediate a rapprochement between them.

These developments are taking place in the developmental environment of China's Belt and Road Initiative, in which all four countries are eager participants. In May, China opened a brand new Embassy building in the Eritrean capital, Asmara. All four countries are planning to attend the Forum on China-Africa Cooperation in Beijing this September.

Economic Integration Marching Forward

With these four nations adopting a win-win approach to relations, the Horn of Africa is poised to become a powerful economic region. Ethiopia, with its large land area and 102 million population, is clearly the motor for rapid development. Somalia, with a population of 14 million, Eritrea with 5 million, and Djibouti's 940,000, need an industrializing country like Ethiopia as their neighbor. The first steps to integration are already in planning. Since the sole port of Djibouti could never serve all of Ethiopia, the first step is to

Port Berbera, the commercial capital of Somaliland, on the coast of the Gulf of Aden, Oct. 11, 2016.

create networks of roads and railways linking the coastal points of Somalia and Eritrea with Ethiopia's regions. This is already happening.

Within two weeks of Afwerki's return to Asmara from Addis Abeba, Eritrea announced the completion of the preliminary refurbishment of its two major ports—Port Massawa in the north of the country and Port Assab in the south. They are ready to again handle Ethiopia's import and export cargoes. Before the two countries went to war in 1998, the two ports were the main ports for Ethiopia. For the last 20 years, the ports have almost become inactive, since they were handling cargo for a country of only 5 million people, while Eritrea had been under sanctions.

The port of Massawa is ideal for handling cargoes to and from northern Ethiopia, especially the city of Mekelle, the capital of Ethiopia's Tigray Regional State. New industrial zones are being developed there, as well as exploitation of mineral and agricultural resources. An Ethiopian delegation led by former Ethiopian Prime Minister Hailemariam Desalegn, and business people who went to Eritrea on the first flight to Asmara in two decades, visited the port.

Before the 1998 war between the two countries, Assab Port had two-thirds of Ethiopia's trade with the world, and had gone through some development, but declined after the war. It also hosts an oil refinery, which has been idle for years.

Addis Abeba University Professor of Public Policy Dr. Costantinos Berhutesfa stated, according to the *Ethiopian Herald,* that Assab can reduce the transportation costs of cargo shipments. He added that with respect to Ethiopia's tremendous potash resources in the Danakil Depression, the Assab Port is ideal for exporting this product, and for establishing a potash-processing plant.

The *Ethiopian Herald* also cited Assistant Professor of Development Economics, Dr. Teshome Adugna: "High transportation cost is one the major setbacks of Ethiopia's export trade, and re-accessing Assab is instrumental in reducing the unit cost of products in the view to penetrate global markets." He said activating the idle oil refinery in Assab would give Ethiopia the opportunity to export processed oil to the world market at better prices.

Somalia also has good seaports. Port Berbera in Somaliland is a major, modern port that Ethiopia wishes to utilize. Ethiopia has acquired a 19% interest in the port, which is run by DP World of Dubai, and is committed to developing the "Berbera Corridor" that will connect Ethiopia to Port Berbera, including transport and energy infrastructure.

Somaliland is officially an autonomous region of Somalia, but it considers itself to be independent, a status that is not recognized by any other nation or international institution. As Somalia stabilizes, relations between the two will have a chance to normalize.

While Berbera is on the north coast of Somalia, there are three other Somali ports available. Port Bosaso is also on the north coast. Two ports are located on the southern coast—the Port of Mogadishu, serving Somalia's capital, which is already connected by road to Ethiopia, and Kismayo, south of Mogadishu.

Somalia now has a way out of its failed-state condition of the past. Its new government is preparing proposals for participation in the Belt and Road Initiative to be presented at the summit of the Forum on China-Africa Cooperation to be held in Beijing in September.

BRICS Reaches Out to Africa, Africa Embraces BRICS

by David Cherry

Aug. 4—Many African leaders are passionate about making Africa into a manufacturing continent—to end its role as simply a raw materials exporter. Never has this passion been more dramatically manifest than in the Outreach Forum of the 10th BRICS Summit of July 25-27 in Johannesburg. The BRICS Summit—on the theme "BRICS in Africa"—was the leadership meeting of the five BRICS member nations, but it also brought together leaders of nine non-member African nations and the chairman of the African Union Commission, for the now traditional BRICS Outreach to the region of the summit host.[1] The government of South Africa, the host, explained that the 2018 Outreach was to ensure "BRICS support for African industrialization and infrastructure development." This is what the African leaders wanted to hear, and their responses were strong.

Xinhua/Wu Changwei

Ship-to-shore cranes at the new container terminal in Walvis Bay, Namibia, Feb. 9, 2018.

The bedtime stories of the old British paradigm, which attempted to divert Africans from industrialization, are losing traction. One of those fairy tales was that African countries can zoom ahead by skipping industrialization and instead marketing "services." Institutions such as the U.S. Agency for International Development (USAID) and the British Department for International Development (DFID) tell African governments that "we are now in the post-industrial stage," in which services dominate the economy, and that Africa can thrive by simply promoting its services sectors—banking in Nigeria, for example, and information technology services in Senegal.

These agencies do not wish to mention, that with the decline of manufacturing in the West, every other aspect of society is also decaying, from infrastructure to education. For example, the estimate of the American Society of Civil Engineers (ASCE) of the cost to repair the worsening infrastructure in the United States has been rising, and is now at $4 trillion dollars. This estimate refers only to infrastructure *repair*, and does not include what it would take for the nation to progress to a higher level.

The same misdirection is evident in the frequent over-emphasis on the "digital revolution," as if software were somehow more important than—or could even supersede—the physical manufacturing processes themselves.

The BRICS Summit shows, however, that African governments are interested in the fundamentals, in manufacturing, even while the full name of the 10th BRICS Summit itself made reference to that software heaven, the "Fourth Industrial Revolution."

Here we report on just some of this commitment to manufacturing expressed by African leaders in the context of the BRICS Summit.

---

1. An additional form of participation in the annual summits is BRICS Plus, which enables the host government to invite a few leaders from around the world. This year South Africa invited Argentina, Indonesia, Egypt, Jamaica, Turkey, and the UN Secretary General to participate. The nine African nations participating under the BRICS Outreach rubric this year were Rwanda, Senegal, Gabon, Uganda, Ethiopia, Togo, Zambia, Namibia, and Angola. In both cases—BRICS Plus and Outreach—South Africa chose countries that are currently chairing regional or international organizations. See http://www.brics2018.org.za/brics-outreach

Namibia: 'Manufacturing Is the Thing'

The President of Namibia, Hage Geingob, discussed BRICS in an interview with Mfundo Mabalane on South Africa's Afro Worldview television. Geingob expressed hope that the New Development Bank of the BRICS is different from the Bretton Woods banks, "so that we can industrialize in Africa." Africa exports its raw materials, he said, and they are processed in Europe, "and then we buy our own goods." But we will put an end to that through BRICS. "We can have one-on-one contact with big powers and we can see how we can actually manufacture in Africa."

Afro Worldview TV

The interview with Hage Geingob, President of Namibia, conducted by Afro Worldview TV's deputy editor Mfundo Mabalane after the summit.

There are powerful, industrialized countries in BRICS, he said, so if we are all pulling in the same direction, less developed countries can be "held under the wings, by South Africa, for instance," when it comes time to negotiate, so we will have more power.

President Geingob addressed criticisms of BRICS by recalling his first visit to China:

I saw all these capitalistic things, so I said, "Oh comrades, what is happening? I see America is here!" And they said "Yes, we have opened up thirty years ago, *but,* whoever comes here, comes on our terms!" And that is the problem in Africa, we allow them. So whoever comes, big or small, to South Africa, to Namibia, we must put our conditions. We told the Chinese, when you come to Namibia, don't bring ordinary wheelbarrow pushers, we have high unemployment....

Namibia must have vocational training, he said, so our people "will use their hands to create things that we will need." He emphasized, "Manufacturing is the thing. All countries in the world, you have to industrialize. Now industrializing also means manufacturing, and therefore to add value to our resources."

Malawi: 'From Consumer to a Producer Economy'

The President of Malawi, Arthur Peter Mutharika, at the BRICS Outreach Forum with African leaders on July 27, told South Africa's Independent Media that "Malawi has a 22-year infrastructure master plan—we need roads, railways and airports, and the creation of the New Development Bank will make it easier for us to access funds in future for infrastructure development."

President Mutharika looked to South Africa to represent the continent: "South Africa has done well to bring African countries on board with regards to BRICS. Africa has a voice and South Africa must speak for us."

"Our biggest challenge," he said, "is to turn our country around from being a consuming to a producing economy, so that we have value-added products to export." Malawi exports raw cotton, for example, but it could be exporting cotton thread or garments.

Angola: 'In the Interest of All Humanity'

Angolan President João Lourenço, in a statement released after the Outreach Forum on July 27, said that the conditions were right for "a concerted strategy of inclusive growth, fight against hunger, reducing the unemployment rate, housing development, improve the people's living conditions, and the creation of partnerships for the integration and industrialization of the entire southern region" of Africa. The BRICS countries had experienced the same stage of economic and social development that Angola is now enduring, "but they managed to make a decisive move toward industrialization."

He called on BRICS to "help Angola overcome the existing constraints to ensure the country's economic development, progress, and people's well-being. We are aware that the collaboration between BRICS and Africa may result in inclusive societies and global partnership in the interest of all humanity."

At the summit, President Lourenço had meetings, as some other presidents did, with China's President Xi Jinping, Russian President Vladimir Putin, Prime Minister of India Narendra Modi, and the President of Turkey, Recep Erdogan.

Nairobi terminal of the new Mombasa-Nairobi rail line.

Uganda: 'Bring Hope to Our Millions'

President of Uganda Yoweri Museveni has been widely quoted as saying, at the Outreach Forum, "Africa is home to more than 1.25 billion people. In East Africa, there are opportunities in fishing, steel, copper, milk, construction, to mention a few. We want the BRICS countries, including South Africa, to invest in railways, construction of roads and other infrastructure development projects in our region." President Museveni said that a partnership with BRICS would bring hope to the more than 168 million people living in East Africa.

Ethiopia: 'BRICS for Space Exploration'

While the BRICS summit was concluding in Johannesburg on July 27, the Xinhua news bureau in Addis Abeba spoke with Gedion Jalata, CEO of an Ethiopian consulting firm, the Center of Excellence International Consult, who said, "BRICS can act as the key financial arm for planned infrastructure projects in Africa.... BRICS could help developing African economies like Ethiopia in future projects like ICT [information and communications technology] development, space exploration and aerospace engineering."

"With South Africa being a member of the BRICS group," he said, "there are bound to be some commitments to support African countries, while the increasing strength of the BRICS bloc means an extended infrastructure commitment for African countries."

Rwanda: 'Revolutionary, More Precious than Money'

In a toast that Rwanda's President Paul Kagame offered to China's President Xi in Johannesburg, President Kagame implicitly acknowledged China's moving spirit in the BRICS. He said,

The growing relationship with China is based as much on mutual respect, as on mutual interests. That is evident, first of all, in your personal commitment to our continent, Mr. President. More generally, China relates to Africa as an equal. We see ourselves as a people on the road to prosperity. China's actions demonstrate that, Mr. President, you see us in the same way. This is a revolutionary posture in world affairs, and it is more precious than money.

Just days earlier, at the conclusion of a July 23 bilateral meeting with President Xi in Kigali, Rwanda, President Kagame said he looked forward to the signing of an MOU in the framework of the Belt and Road Initiative. He laid out his vision of the future of Africa's economy, which BRICS will have a great role to play in bringing into being. He said in part:

This [cooperation with China] presents new opportunities for Rwanda, the region, and our continent as a whole. Rwanda's location, at the convergence of western and central African regional blocs, presents opportunities to become the land-

Xinhua/CGC

The Muyanza Dam in Rwanda, built by China Geo-Engineering Corp., Feb. 16, 2018.

Xinhua/Li Sibo

Beijing Automotive Industry Corporation shows off the first automobile produced at its plant in Port Elizabeth, South Africa. July 24, 2018.

opment of industrial parks, and energy. As China moves towards shifting its production structure, moving up the technology value chain through its "Made in China 2025" policy, Rwanda could strategically position itself to acquire some of its primary industries, in sectors such as automobile assembling plants, electronic products, garment, and shoe-making.

I, once again, wish to congratulate China for the partnership in building the recently opened Djibouti International Free Trade Zone. I was there, myself, to witness that, and encourage the same company, China Merchants Holdings, a subsidiary of China Merchants Group, to invest in free trade zones in Rwanda.

bridge in the heart of Africa. Through projects such as a standard gauge railway, the interior of Africa will be linked to the coast, thereby contributing to deeper integration of African economies and beyond.

We welcome businesses from China to invest in Rwanda, especially in manufacturing, development of industrial parks, and energy. As

All of the African nations represented in this survey have already had direct experience, in their own countries, of the new spirit that has animated China especially since it announced its Belt and Road Initiative in September and October 2013. It is this experience that has prepared the way for these nations' reception of the BRICS and its vision.

Gateway to Our Galaxy: New Horizons Revisited

by Janet G. West

Author's note: About three years ago, EIR reported on some of the initial findings of the New Horizons flyby of Pluto on July 14, 2015. This is intended to augment that discussion.

"Ah, but a man's reach should exceed his grasp; Or what's a Heaven for?"

—*Robert Browning*

July 29—The extraordinary New Horizons mission *would not have occurred*, were it not for the mindset—the perseverance, leadership and at times, sheer determination—of the scientists who organized the project, as well as the thousands of engineers, technicians, analysts and others who collaborated to ensure its success. That story is nearly as fascinating and dramatic as the mission to Pluto itself.[1]

By the 1980s, these scientists realized that although there were NASA missions to the planets, there were none planned for the exploration of Pluto. Being planetary scientists who liked challenges, Pluto offered enticing mysteries for them—even without the advantages of what could be seen with the Hubble telescope later—and an informal grouping of "Plutophiles" formed. The timing of Pluto's orbit lent some urgency to the effort, since it was on a trajectory of its closest approach to the Sun; a mission would have to be launched in time to take advantage of this.

The New Horizons (NH) spacecraft was launched on January 19, 2006, with the fastest launch speed of any spacecraft, reaching the orbit of the Moon in just nine hours. It is the first and only mission planned to explore Pluto and the Kuiper Belt. Travelling with an average speed of 32,000 mph, it didn't arrive near Pluto for its now-famous flyby until nearly 10 years after its launch, at which time it delivered stunning pictures of Pluto and its moons. Its mission has been extended by NASA, so it will continue to explore new celestial bodies; during the upcoming New Year's Day 2019, it will be flying by the Kuiper Belt Object 2014 MU69 (recently unofficially renamed "Ultima Thule"[2]), which is another *one billion miles* beyond Pluto.

---

1. Stern, Alan and Grinspoon, David. *Chasing New Horizons: Inside the Epic First Mission to Pluto*. Picador. 2018.

2. "*Thule*" was the name given by ancient Greeks of a mythical place or island that was the furthest north; *Ultima Thule* would mean "beyond the frontiers of the known world."

A Galactic Orientation

Before looking at the New Horizons mission more closely, we first need to change our perspective of the ordering principle of our science: the "norm" has been to start from the small (our Earth), and gradually to the large (the Moon, the Sun, the planets, etc.) However, if you step out under a clear night sky, away from city lights, what is the largest structure you see? The Milky Way!—stretching from horizon to horizon. It is our galaxy, which—as we're beginning to discover increasingly—determines some of our weather and other activity, as our solar system moves in its orbit.

Astronomy was mankind's first science. Prehistoric man navigated the trackless oceans by understanding the diurnal, seasonal and longer cyclical changes in the paths of the heavenly bodies above. The points and circles we now draw on our globes—the equator, the tropics, and the poles, for example—were first drawn on the celestial sphere, before being copied down onto Earth's surface much later. The Greeks knew the locations of the poles, and the climate of the Arctic and Antarctic, without ever having been to either pole—we didn't get there until the Twentieth Century. Indeed, the word "climate" is just the Greek word for the inclination of the Sun's rays.

In our mind's eye, from the celestial sphere we move to the larger scale of the galaxy. On its journey of 230 million years in orbit within the Milky Way, our solar system is affected by diverse galactic environments, such as when it moves "north" and "south" of the galactic plane, as well as other influences. Right now, our solar system is moving through a Local Interstellar Cloud which may have unpredictable effects on our weather.[3] There is a correlation between Ice Ages on Earth, and the passage of our solar system through the Milky Way's spiral arms. Also, all the planets are affected by the solar wind; scientists are still uncovering how it and cosmic radiation impact and interact with the solar system; how they drive weather; how geological events like volcanoes are affected, and so forth.

Keplerian Principles:
Towards a New Astronomy

To examine and challenge one's own axioms and assumptions is one of the hallmarks of true science; a true scientist is happy to have erroneous hypotheses over-turned. Scientists are constantly developing hypotheses and then overthrowing them with newer, less imperfect hypotheses about the nature of the Universe. In the words of one delighted scientist, "[What we've found on Pluto]…has inspired me! It showed me just how wrong I could be!" It is often through an apparent "dissonance" or "anomaly," that true science makes progress.

The Universe is usually described in such a way that assumes the validity of the Second Law of Thermodynamics, but this view doesn't align with the development of Earth's biosphere or explain the existence of man. Lyndon H. LaRouche, in his 1988 autobiography *The Power of Reason* talks about his development of a science of physical economy based on man's creative capabilities and the tendency of the Universe to be anti-entropic (a method which produces his accurate economic forecasting). LaRouche said in that book, "A universe based on principles of winding down, could not have come into existence in the first place."

The standard description for the formation of our solar system starts with a broad rotating disk of lumpy matter, and larger clumps would attract smaller clumps, and increase in size solely due to rocks banging into each other. This friction would heat up the rocky clumps. They would get larger and larger until gravity took over and they began clearing out the area around them. Under this model, the asteroid belt and Kuiper Belt are considered to be the "leftovers" from this process. We need a new astronomy to meet the challenges of expanded space exploration. It takes more than geometry and calculations to think about the solar system and the galaxy. One must use one's mind eye to take a step out into space at a point at infinity; this is what early astronomers had to do to understand the motion of the heavens—it goes beyond the senses. Just as the introduction of the point at infinity on the horizon revolutionized the world of art, so too can a "long perspective" of the solar system and our galaxy reshape astronomy.[4]

Most science books will tell you who discovered what and when, but they rarely tell you the method by which the discovery was made, but it's the method which is most important. As Louis Pasteur once observed, "Chance favors only the prepared mind."

---

3. https://science.nasa.gov/science-news/science-at-nasa/2009/23dec_voyager.

4. Perspective was first developed rigorously by Filippo Brunelleschi (1377-1446) and Leon Battista Alberti (1404-72) as part of the Golden Renaissance; increasing the powers of artists, architects and engineers, as well as the intellectual powers of the average person.

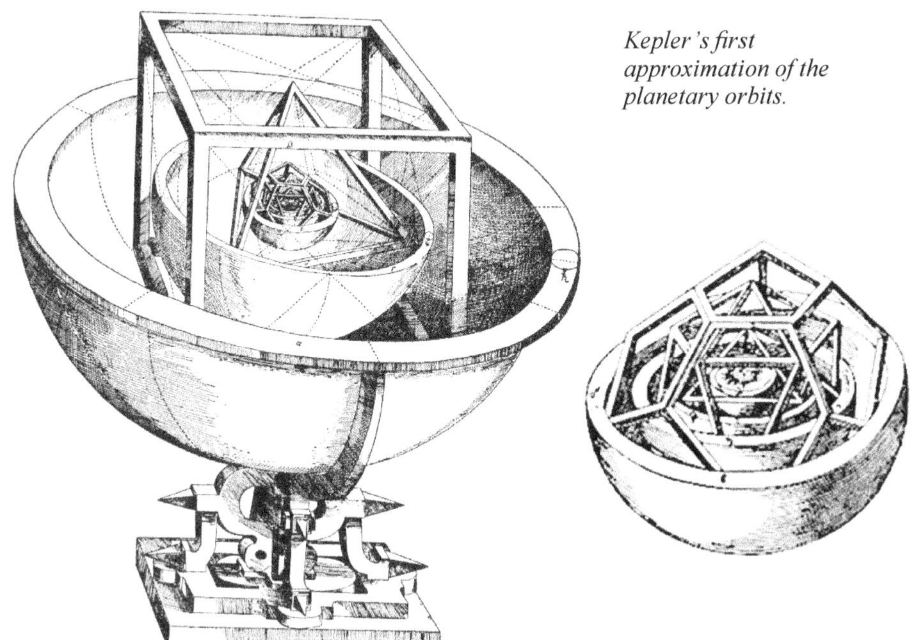

Kepler's first approximation of the planetary orbits.

Johannes Kepler was still a university student when he obtained Copernicus' book which revived Aristarchus' understanding that the planets orbit the Sun. Kepler recognized that Copernicus' work left the important problems still unanswered, and hypothesized that the planetary orbits were determined by concentric spheres circumscribed around, and inscribed within, the five nested Platonic solids. This was not a "model," as contemporary neo-Babylonian thinking would insist, but rather an hypothesis—later proven by Karl Gauss with the case of the asteroid Ceres—concerning the *cause* for the given orbits. From the ancient Pythagoreans, to Plato's *Timaeus*, Kepler, Gauss, Riemann, Planck and Einstein, scientific thought worthy of that name has always known that space-time is not a mere empty container, but rather has a structure.

The ancient Greeks understood that the fact itself that only these five regular solids can be constructed, is a feature of the structure of space—and the planetary orbits are determined by the structure of space. Kepler's later, refined hypothesis included the harmonic relationships among the orbits of the planets. He discovered that the relationships between the perihelion and aphelion of the orbits of adjacent planets could be translated into musical notes. For example, the asteroid belt between Mars and Jupiter represents the note of F#, a dissonance within the C major scale[5] so great that no planet could form.

Through some of his thoughts, you may understand better that Kepler wasn't a "cold, calculating mathematician":

We do not ask for what useful purpose the birds sing, for song is their pleasure since they were created for singing. Similarly, we ought not to ask why the human mind troubles to fathom the secrets of the heavens…The diversity of the phenomena of Nature is so great, and the treasures hidden in the heavens so rich, precisely in order the human mind shall never be lacking in fresh nourishment.[6]

In the case of calculating Mars' orbit, Kepler didn't just rely on his senses, which told him that Mars made a loop (retrograde motion) in its transit in the sky; Kepler's method included exhaustive calculations of Earth's and Mars' orbits, but he also did something remarkable: in his mind's eye, he "viewed" the orbits from the point of view of the Sun, and then from Mars, looking back at Earth's orbit, in order to fully understand not just the calculations, but the *relationships* between the Sun and the planets. Kepler also challenged future scientists to improve upon his system. Kepler saw no dichotomy between geometry and music; astronomy and God:

The heavenly bodies are nothing but a continuous song for several voices (perceived by the intellect, not by the ear); a music which…sets landmarks in the immeasurable flow of time. It is therefore, no longer surprising that man, in imi-

---

5. *Manual on the Rudiments of Tuning and Registration, Book I.* The Schiller Institute, 1992.
6. *Mysterium Cosmographicum.*

tation of his creator, has at last discovered the art of figured song, which was unknown to the ancients. Man wanted to reproduce the continuity of cosmic time…to obtain a sample test of the delight of the Divine Creator in His works, and to partake of his joy by making music in the imitation of God.

In the same tradition, in an article addressing the insidious effect of philosophical reductionism (empiricism) on physical science, Lyndon LaRouche observed:

Currently, our best knowledge is that the Solar System began as a fast-spinning, youthfully exuberant solitary Sun in the universe at large. According to Kepler's principles, this young Sun spun off some part of its material into a disk orbiting the Sun itself. If we assume polarized nuclear fusion occurring within that disk, then it were possible for polarized fusion, and, presumably, only polarized fusion, to have generated the observed periodic table of the Solar System. That fusion-generated material from the disk would have been "fractionally distilled" into approximately the Platonic orbits defined by Kepler. Then, according to Gauss's reading of the matter, the elliptical-harmonic characteristics of the orbit would have "condensed" the material distributed along each orbit into relevant planets and their moons. The crucial view of this hypothesis was provided by Gauss's proof of Kepler's case for the self-fractured missing planet, the debris known as the Asteroid belt.

Such Kepler-Gauss-et al. conclusions are in accord with the primary characteristics of what I have summarily described as Vernadsky's systemic biogeochemical view of the universe. In other words, the argument is, that the universe is created as an intrinsically self-developing universe, in a process of development expressed, inclusively, by built-in generation of more highly differentiated states of self-organization. Additionally, that the anti-entropic principle of cognition (*noësis*) already existed in that universe "from the beginning," but could be expressed as man only under the emergence of certain new, lawfully generated states of local organization of the universe as part of the universe's overall, anti-entropic self-development. Since the anti-entropic principles of life and *noësis* are of a universal quality inhering in a multiply-connected universe, the universe was always anti-entropic as a whole. Man's manifest power to increase his willful control over the universe through nothing other than *noësis*, demonstrates this experimentally. Such is the work of epistemology; no ideas are legitimate, unless the necessity of their coming into being is demonstrated from an experimental standpoint.[7]

These *noetic* powers of the human mind, as identified by the great geobiochemist V.I. Vernadsky, and developed in-depth by LaRouche's writings on economics, philosophy and creativity, are that which distinguish human beings from the beasts, and increase man's powers over nature.

There have been other scientists who have also promoted this view of mankind, and their writings should be revived for future space missions. In the 1950s, the late famous scientist Krafft Ehricke promoted the idea of the "extraterrestrial imperative"—the necessity for man to explore space and develop its resources. Among other accomplishments, Ehricke worked on the first liquid-hydrogen-fueled rocket that would be the basis for the Saturn V rocket and was the chief scientist for the Space Systems Division of North American Aviation (later Rockwell International) in the 1960s and into the 1970s.

He outlined his Three Laws of Astronautics (1957):

• **First Law:** Nobody and nothing under the natural laws of this universe impose any limitations on man except man himself.

• **Second Law:** Not only the Earth, but the entire Solar System, and as much as the universe as he can reach under the laws of nature, are man's rightful field of activity.

• **Third Law:** By expanding through the universe, man fulfills his destiny as an element of life, endowed with the power of reason and the wisdom of the moral law within himself.

Krafft Ehricke made many profound contributions to the exploration of space and typifies the hopeful perspective that can guide a mission orientation for our solar system and beyond.

---

7. LaRouche, Jr., Lyndon H.; *Visualizing the Complex Domain*, EIR 2003.

The Problem with Science Today

It will be the task of a future work to address the enormous targetted assault on the American people in the wake of World War II, attacking nuclear energy and radiation through movies and popular culture. Of course, there are dangers associated with radiation (as well as benefits), but tales of giant ants, moths, and other monsters produced by atomic testing go beyond the pale.

However, the reality of Sputnik smacked Americans out of their stupor, awakening a renewed interest in science and increased respect for scientists and engineers. President John Kennedy's famous speech of 1962 rallied the nation to send astronauts to the moon and return them safely back to Earth:

> We choose to go to the moon in this decade and do the other things, not because they are easy, but because they are hard, because that goal will serve to organize and measure the best of our energies and skills, because that challenge is one that we are willing to accept, one we are unwilling to postpone, and one which we intend to win, and the others, too.[8]

This mission injected new energy into the scientific community and rallied the educational institutions to expedite the development of engineering and other scientific disciplines. The successful missions also created a blooming of optimism, in America and around the world.

When American astronauts first landed on the Moon, the entire world celebrated the accomplishment; an estimated 600 million people watched the landing via television, and more than a billion listened by radio. Soon after their return to Earth, they visited many nations as part of a worldwide Goodwill Tour, and they remarked that **no one** they met, no matter what country they were in, would say, "The Americans did it"; it was always "*WE* did it!" Neil Armstrong's famous quote, "One small step for a man, one giant leap for mankind," would be echoed by other Apollo astronauts: the consensus was, "We did this for all mankind." A great promising era opened up.

But, then came the Rock-Drug-Sex Counterculture/New Age Movement (organized and deployed by the British oligarchy), and for the most part, our population capitulated; even our best scientists have been infected with the spores from this cultural slime-mold.

At the same time, the idea of "entropy is the law of the Universe," as promoted by Norbert Wiener, was heavily propagandized on all levels:

> Sooner or later we shall die, and it is highly probable that the whole universe around us will die the heat death. We are immersed in a life in which the world as a whole obeys the second law of thermodynamics; confusion increases and order decreases....[9]

Our problem is not so much the environmentalists and "zero-growthers"— our Achilles heel is the lack of scientific thinking among most Americans, and a certain kind of moral and intellectual cowardice. Anyone at least as smart as a caveman could surmise the agenda of "environmentalism": genocide against humanity. Why weren't the environmentalists run out of town on a rail, by most citizens, at the very start?[10] Who benefits from duping much of the Western world to perform, in effect, a mass lobotomy?

And, don't be fooled into thinking that they care about "Mother Earth." There are many examples, but an egregious one is that *just one* "solar plant" kills up to 6,000 birds annually, since it's built *right in the path* of the Pacific Flyway— one of the major migratory pathways for birds.[11] Due to the power of the sun's concentrated rays, as the birds fly over the "plant," they are incinerated instantly, leaving little plumes of smoke wafting in the wind. And, wind turbines kill upwards of 328,000 birds and up to 900,000 bats annually. (Any farmer can tell you how important and useful bats are— some for pest control and some for pollination, depending on species.)

Why give any credence to some pagan who may worship the Winter Solstice, but couldn't begin to tell you what a solstice is? Just for fun, ask one of these dimwits some time to draw out the orbit of the Earth, and show you where, when and why the solstice occurs.

Many scientists, or nominal scientists, have capitulated to this mindset, giving lip-service to the second law of thermodynamics; to "climate change"[12] or what-

---

8. https://er.jsc.nasa.gov/seh/ricetalk.htm.

9. Norbert Weiner, *The Human Use of Human Beings*, USA 1950

10. Locals in Alberta, Canada rightly mocked and ridiculed a famous Hollywood actor when, while filming on location, he warned that the warm seasonal Chinook winds "were a sign of climate change"

11. The Ivanpah Solar Plant; https://www.scientificamerican.com/article/solar-farms-threaten-birds/

12. Wasn't it "global cooling" in the 1970s? Then, the "Ozone hole,"

ever is the current "crisis," with a heteronomic "me, first" mentality for a perceived limited resource—funding. The unifying conception of a national mission—such as we saw under the Kennedy Space Program—is nowhere to be found.

The level of some of these "scientists" reminds one of the academy of "researchers" found in Jonathan Swift's *Gulliver's Travels*:

> The first man I saw was of a meagre aspect, with sooty hands and face, his hair and beard long, ragged, and singed in several places. His clothes, shirt, and skin, were all of the same colour. He has been eight years upon a project for extracting sunbeams out of cucumbers, which were to be put in phials hermetically sealed, and let out to warm the air in raw inclement summers....
>
> I went into another chamber, but was ready to hasten back, being almost overcome with a horrible stink. My conductor pressed me forward, conjuring me in a whisper "to give no offence, which would be highly resented"; and therefore I durst not so much as stop my nose. The projector of this cell was the most ancient student of the academy; his face and beard were of a pale yellow; his hands and clothes daubed over with filth. When I was presented to him, he gave me a close embrace, a compliment I could well have excused. His employment, from his first coming into the academy, was an operation to reduce human excrement to its original food, by separating the several parts, removing the tincture which it receives from the gall, making the odour exhale, and scumming off the saliva.[13] [*sic*]

It is time to leave the land of the Lilliputians behind, and think like human beings again.

A Sense of Perspective

For the purposes of making more knowable to the reader the magnitude of the New Horizons mission, we'll describe some of the relationships within our solar system.

Pluto is smaller than our Moon and possesses about the same surface area as Russia. It is on average 3.6 billion miles from the Earth, and its orbit is highly elliptical

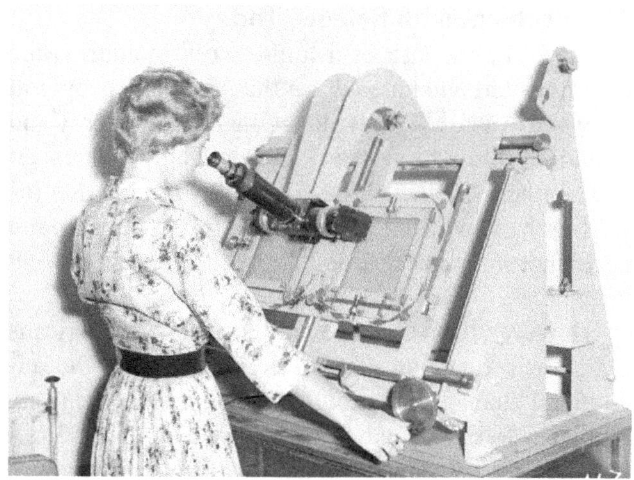

Blink comparator.

(2.6 billion miles from the Sun at the perihelion and about 4.6 billion at the aphelion), as well as cutting at an oblique plane relative to the plane of the other planets' orbits. Its moons are Charon, Styx, Nix, Kerberos and Hydra. Although there's been some controversy as to whether or not it's a planet, a new definition has been developed to include Pluto as a dwarf planet, and possibly even a "binary planet," due to its interaction with its closest moon, Charon.

Pluto was discovered in 1939, by Clyde Tombaugh, a farmer who was a self-taught astronomer; he had built telescopes on his farm, and after some entreaties to the Lowell Observatory in Arizona, was offered an opportunity to work there.

There had been a search for a "Planet X" for many years, due to observed perturbations of Neptune's orbit, and he took up the search. Tirelessly, night after night for nearly a year, he took pictures of a particular spot in the night sky (where "Planet X" was thought to be), using an instrument called a blink comparator. By his perseverance, he noted a faint object moving against the background of stars—he had discovered Pluto![14] The method he developed for scanning the star field is still used today by astronomers. It is altogether fitting that some of his ashes fly onboard New Horizons, in honor of his discovery of the ninth planet.

We're all familiar with the classroom-type poster of the solar system, and the planets neatly lined up to show their "relative sizes." But, it were better to take a galactic

---

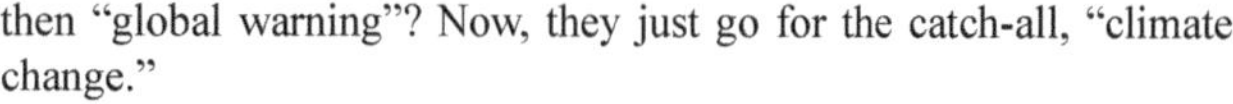

then "global warning"? Now, they just go for the catch-all, "climate change."

13. *Gulliver's Travels*; first published in Ireland, 1726.

14. John Keats' sonnet, "*On First Looking into Chapman's Homer*," expresses this wonder of discovery beautifully; this very well could have been how Tombaugh felt for some minutes after the discovery, when he was the only person on Earth to know that 'Planet X' had been found.

step back in order to review the relative sizes and distances of the planets in our solar system. Imagine the sun to be the size of a soccer ball, sitting on the goal line of a football field. Earth would be around the 26-yard line, and about a quarter inch in diameter. Going past Mars and the asteroid belt, we find Jupiter, 135 yards away from the "sun," and about the size of a grape; going onwards to Neptune (pea-sized) we arrive at it nearly eight football fields away from the soccer-sun (or about 2,880 feet—slightly over one-half mile). We would have to travel another *17 miles beyond Neptune,* to reach pea-sized Pluto.

Now, going back up to its true, real-life scale, imagine the entire solar system in motion, and having the task to engineer a spacecraft about the size of a grand piano that had to be launched within a narrow time window, fly into the correct trajectory around Jupiter to get a gravity-assist, travelling at 32,000 mph, and successfully take scientific measurements in a flyby of Pluto lasting only a matter of hours, with a 9-hour round-trip communication link, all within NASA's parameters and budget, using new technologies in a first-ever (and "one shot") attempt to reach the outer reaches of our solar system. And, it had to get there within a 9 minute window on either side! Now, you have some perspective as to the true magnitude of this project.

'Why *Not* Us? Why Not *Now*?'

It's beyond the scope of this article to detail the fourteen-year-long struggle to organize, fund and launch the Pluto mission, but since it is vital to understand, a brief history is included. The leading scientists have been Alan Stern, Fran Bagenal, Ralph McNutt, Marc Buie, and William McKinnon. There are many more who lent their efforts to the mission, too numerous to mention here, but their dedication to the mission is recognized.

Had we a different culture and economics in this country—the economics of life, as developed by physical economist Lyndon H. LaRouche, Jr.—and the optimistic culture of our past (that of the landing on the Moon) and our hopeful future (the Spirit of the New Silk Road)—it were possible that there would have been no need for such a struggle for funding. There need be none in the future, given a revival of American System economics.

The scientists who have addressed various public forums and colloquiums have emphasized that the mission "takes a team"; but not only in terms of personnel. The mission depended heavily on numerous agencies, and most importantly, the Hubble telescope and the Deep Space Network.

Before 1990, a mission to Pluto wasn't even a gleam in NASA's eye. The idea first came into being in 1989, when Alan Stern and some fellow "Plutophiles" gathered after a conference of the American Geophysical Union (AGU) in Baltimore, MD at a local restaurant. There, Stern had the audacity to propose, "We need a mission to Pluto!" He understood that part of the urgency lay in the timing of the orbit of Pluto, and various other alignments of the planets, such as Jupiter, so that the spacecraft could take advantage of a "gravity assist" from Jupiter. He began to organize the scientific community.

There were six different versions of the Pluto mission from 1989 to 2001 (NH is the sixth and final version). With each version, the team was asked to meet a new parameter: bigger, smaller, more instruments; budgets were cut, goalposts moved; redundant analysis of each instrument; etc. Each time, the team rose to the occasion and overcame the challenges, much as a great general will outflank the enemy, again and again, to reach the objective.

In 1995, the team had to contend with budget considerations, and they searched for ways to reduce the costs of a launch as much as possible. The team needed to design a craft with the smallest mass possible. The mission also required a very powerful rocket. Understanding that relations between the U.S. and Russia were beginning to thaw, Stern saw an opportunity. In a gutsy move, he decided—on his own—to travel to Russia to meet with Alec Galeev, head of the Space Research Institute in Moscow, to explore the possibility of Russian assistance with a launch, holding out the carrot that Russia could include a probe, so that Russia could claim that it was the first nation to touch Pluto. But, in 1996, for various reasons the Russians decided against providing a no-cost launch. (And, no wonder—everybody knows "there ain't no such thing as a free launch.")

Finally, the last straw came when—after an intense period of preparation, testing, and competition with the Jet Propulsion Laboratory (JPL) for the Pluto mission contract—the incoming 2001 Bush administration zeroed-out the budget. Stamatios "Tom" Krimigis, the head of the Space Science Department at the Johns Hopkins University Applied Physics Laboratory, responded to the crisis with something like, "*It's time to break some legs!*"[15] He put in a call to Sen. Barbara Mi-

---

15. Stern and Grinspoon, note 1.

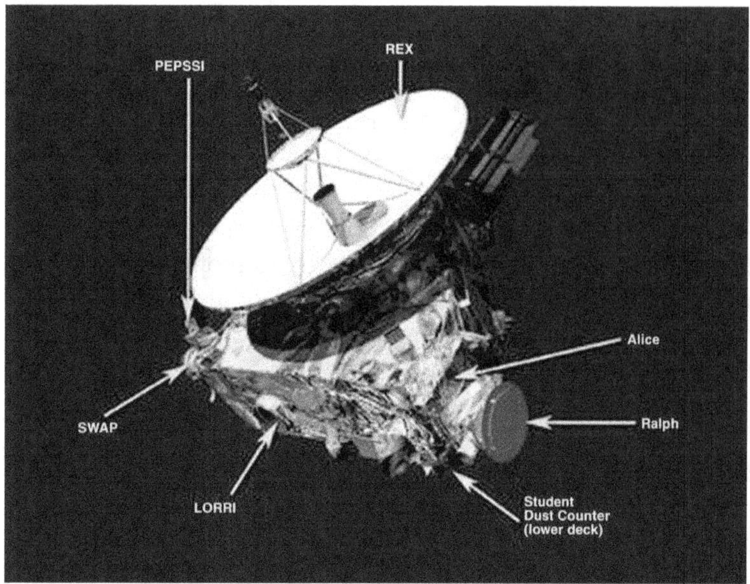

New Horizons Spacecraft 3.

kulski, then chair of the Senate Appropriations Committee. She virtually ordered NASA to fund the Pluto project, and the project moved forward. We need more such scientists willing to put pressure on Congress for the right reasons.

The mission got underway, and Alan Stern, chosen to be the Principal Investigator, had the honor of naming the mission. As he relates in his book, he wanted something inspiring and hopeful, and being inspired himself while on a run in Colorado, as he set his eyes upon the enchanting horizon outlining the Rocky Mountains, he struck upon, "New Horizons."

'Though She Be but Little, She is Fierce!'

The NH spacecraft is about the size and shape of a grand piano, and she is packed with scientific instruments:

Ralph: Visible and infrared imager/spectrometer; provides color, composition and thermal maps.

Alice: Ultraviolet imaging spectrometer; analyzes composition and structure of Pluto's atmosphere and looks for atmospheres around Charon and Kuiper Belt Objects (KBOs).[16]

REX: (Radio Science Experiment) Measures atmospheric composition and temperature; passive radiometer.

LORRI: (Long Range Reconnaissance Imager) Telescopic camera; obtains encounter data at long dis-

tances, maps Pluto's far side and provides high resolution geologic data.

SWAP: (Solar Wind Around Pluto) Solar wind and plasma spectrometer; measures atmospheric "escape rate" and observes Pluto's interaction with solar wind.

PEPSSI: (Pluto Energetic Particle Spectrometer Science Investigation) Energetic particle spectrometer; measures the composition and density of plasma (ions) escaping from Pluto's atmosphere.

SDC: (Student Dust Counter) Built and operated by students; measures the space dust peppering New Horizons during its voyage across the solar system.[17]

The spacecraft is powered by—what else?—*plutonium*! "Electrical power for the New Horizons mission … is furnished by a single radioisotope thermoelectric generator (RTG), which transforms the heat from the natural radioactive decay of plutonium dioxide fuel into electricity."[18]

It began with 240 watts of power at launch; if all the instruments were to be turned on at once (which Mission Control wouldn't do), they would use *30 watts*! (Think of what we could do with fusion-powered rockets!)

'Like Nothing Else in the Solar System'

After the flyby, the first pictures were breathtaking; but the real test would be whether NH relayed the signal that it had survived the flyby intact. It would be 14 hours before the team would know. Then came Mission Operations Manager Alice Bowman's calm confirmation: "We are in lock with telemetry with the spacecraft.… We've received data at the Pluto system, and we're outbound from Pluto." The full data set would take 15 months to be transmitted.[19]

Due to the embedded assumption that entropy is the law of the universe, the prevailing view has been that small planets should cool off faster than the big planets. It was fully expected that Pluto was a cold, dead planet.

Initial hypotheses about Pluto indicated that it was too small and cold to have an atmosphere; and even if it did have an atmosphere, the computer models predicted it to be unsubstantial. Computer models are notoriously

---

16. Ralph and Alice are named after "The Honeymooners" television series of the 1950's.

17. www.nasa.gov/mission_pages/newhorizons/spacecraft/index.html.

18. https://rps.nasa.gov/missions/7/new-horizons/.

19. Stern and Grinspoon, note 1.

First close-up picture of Pluto.

Colorized photo of Pluto.

wrong, because the axioms of entropy are built into the calculations. No computer can account for the non-linear effects expressed by even non-living processes.

Atmosphere on Pluto was first detected in 1988 by the Kuiper Airborne Observatory; the pictures from NH showed a complex atmosphere with *well-organized layers* and haze, up to 100 miles thick! Confirming the 1988 findings, after the flyby, NH rotated to photograph a dark Pluto backlit by the sun—a bright blue haze encircled the planet. The color is due to complex organic molecules, called *tholins*, which are reddish-brown when they drop to the surface, but scatter blue light when in the atmosphere. Tholins are thought to contain some of the chemical precursors of life. This also explains the reddish-brown coloration of the older portions of the planet's surface. Scientists associated with the mission were thrilled, since this also indicates weather on Pluto.

Thanks to other missions, we've been able to study the weather on other planets, such as Jupiter, Saturn and Neptune; each one is a study in anomalies and unexplained phenomena. Although we know of the 11-year sunspot activity cycle on our Sun, and that it affects weather, it doesn't explain the intense and dynamic weather so distant from the sun. What role might the solar wind play? What might UV and infrared light reveal about these weather systems? Think of the solar system as an actual system—not just a conglomeration of planets like billiard balls—and the complicated interactions between orbit, tilt of the planet, solar activity, galactic cycles and other influences yet unknown, from a principle of anti-entropy; that is, a demonstrable tendency of the Universe towards increased order, increased energy throughput, as well as differentiation.

"Who would have expected a blue sky in the Kuiper Belt?" New Horizons principal investigator Alan Stern of the Southwest Research Institute (SwRI) in Boulder, Colorado, said in a statement. "It's glorious."[20]

---

20. www.space.com/18564-pluto-atmosphere.html.

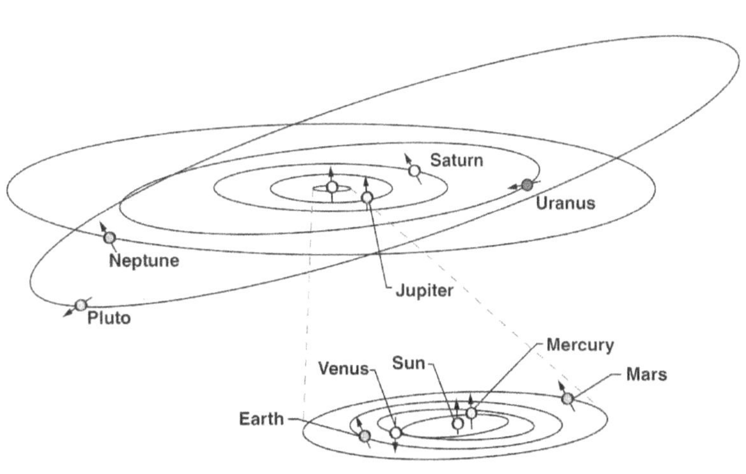

Orbits of the planets.

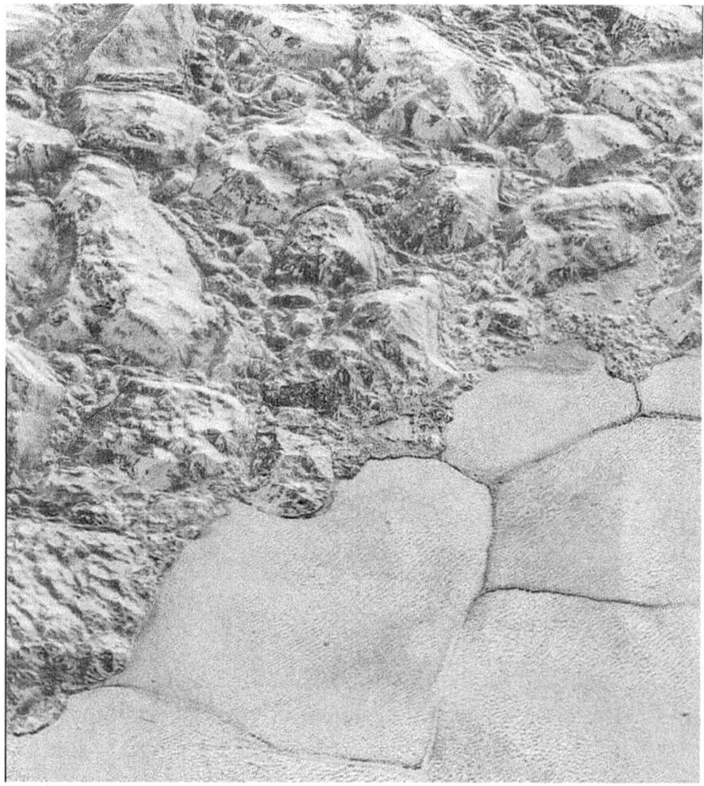

Dunes at the top, convection cells at bottom, on Pluto.

The weather and seasons on Pluto are complicated and will require research for years to come. Pluto's orbit takes 248 years for one circuit around the sun and is at an oblique angle to the rest of the solar system; one Pluto day is 6.4 Earth days; it has a retrograde rotation, and its axis varies between 102 and 126 degrees. And, like many planets, the axis experiences precession.

Add into this the complex nature of the binary rotation between Pluto and Charon, and it adds up to a very elaborate and dynamic weather system.[21]

The atmosphere of Pluto also has an intricate relationship with the solar wind; during portions of the year as different areas of Pluto are exposed to it, the atmosphere can vary in size and pressure. As the planet warms, the atmosphere rises and thickens; at other points, it "snows" onto the surface. How might this phenomenon affect geology?

In terms of surface features, what immediately gripped the attention of the scientists was the broad white heart-shaped feature (informally named "*Tombaugh Regio*," and the smaller "*Sputnik Planium*"). It's

astonishing to realize that there are *no craters* in this region; yet this planet is at least 4 billion years old, and cosmic objects have hit it continually, just as our Moon has been similarly bombarded! Scientists hypothesized that "something" was smoothing over the area—but what?

Looking closer, they found large hexagonal-shaped cells (about a mile across) that were determined to be convection cells. It is thought that the icy nitrogen surface is "boiling"—albeit slowly—and this churning is renewing the surface, smoothing over any craters. Scientists hypothesize that there's a subterranean ocean of liquid water; as the water rises, it freezes. The physics of freezing water is counter-intuitive: as water freezes, it releases latent heat energy to the surrounding environment. This is enough heat—just a few degrees—to cause the nitrogen to churn.

Another phenomenon—only seen on the *Sputnik Planium*—are hundreds of "pock marks" (that aren't impact craters), that seem to follow the flow of a huge glacier, but scientists are unsure how they are created. Now, the possibility of active geologic activity within this dwarf planet is being explored, since there's a huge variety of terrain. In reviewing the various geological features, Alan Stern joyfully exclaimed, "Everywhere we look, we find puzzles!"

There's a feature on the surface which appears to be a huge shield volcano. But—what could be powering it? Known as Wright Mons, it measures about 90 miles in diameter and about 2.5 miles high! Since it only has one large crater, scientists believe that there has been recent flow smoothing out other craters—but with a flow of what?

On another part of the hemisphere, there's an area of huge, blade-like ice mountains, oriented in a similar direction, ranging up to about 1,500 feet in height. Recent research indicates that they are made of methane ice that sublimates from the atmosphere and may have a base of water ice. It's still unknown why they have such sharp features, instead of being the expected nondescript blobs.

There are also discoveries on the largest of Pluto's moons, Charon. Its polar cap has a "stain," the reddish-brown indicating the presence of tholins. But Charon has no atmosphere. The current hypothesis is that at particular times during Pluto's orbit, some of the tholins in Pluto's atmosphere are transferred to Charon, but the mechanism is unknown.

---

21. They are mutually tidally locked; the same surface of each faces the other as they rotate around a common center.

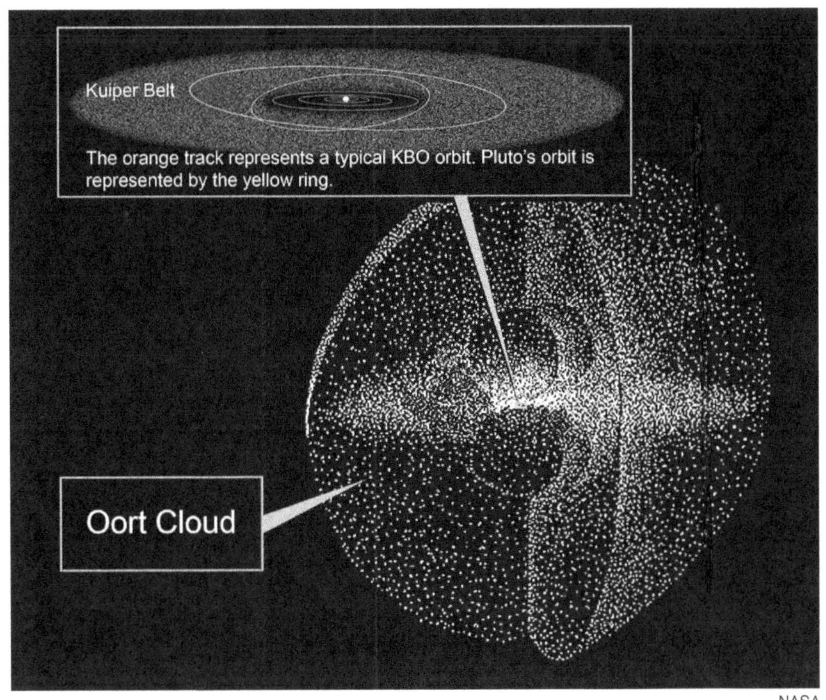

Kuiper Belt and Oort Cloud.

The original specifications for the flyby had it set for 7,800 miles above the planet's surface; it arrived 83 seconds early, and 50 miles lower than planned—after a trip of 3 billion miles and 9.5 years! The flyby was covered on the front page of 458 newspapers, on all seven continents (yes, even Antarctica). New Horizons performed flawlessly.

One scientist in particular, Richard Binzel of MIT, summarized it enthusiastically, "Pluto isn't 'amazing'—Pluto is *ridiculously*, fantastically complex—even more than we imagined!"

The Kuiper Belt and Oort Cloud

Up until recently, the solar system was divided into two main regions: the inner "rocky" planets, and the four outer "gas giants," divided by the asteroid belt.[22] When it dawned on key administrators that Pluto and the Kuiper Belt represented a third, new zone of the solar system—this created excitement and renewed interest in the NH mission.

Predicted to exist in the 1950s by Gerard Kuiper, this is a belt which is billions of miles wide containing millions of comets, thousands of other icy objects and hundreds of dwarf planets. It is thought that this is the region from which many comets originate, and contains

the oldest objects in our solar system, going back to its inception. Study of this region, it is thought, may be able to begin to answer questions surrounding the origins of our solar system. The next object of study of NH, the Kuiper Belt Object 2014 MU69, has never been a comet, and as Alan Stern said with exuberance in a 2016 presentation, "[It will be] the most pristine relic of the solar system formation ever explored, and the flyby will be closer than Pluto...."

Beyond the Kuiper belt, and still theoretical—is believed to be the Oort Cloud, named after the Dutch astronomer, Jan Oort, who hypothesized its existence in 1950; instead of another "belt" or "zone," the Oort Cloud is thought to be a spherical reservoir of icy celestial bodies—the nuclei of long-range comets—representing the very edges of the reach of our sun's gravitational field, and well beyond the heliosphere; the radius is estimated at 4.6 trillion miles beyond the Kuiper Belt.

Voyager I (launched in 1977) is still operational and travelling at about a million miles per day; it will take over 1,200 years to reach the Oort Cloud (if it exists), and over 12,000 years to pass through it. The latest estimates as to the number of objects in the Oort Cloud are in the range of 2 trillion, but it could be higher.

What we do know is the general structure of the phenomenon at the far reaches of the heliosphere, thanks to Voyager I and Voyager II. At the very edges of the heliopause (where our system pushes against the interstellar wind), scientists are discovering a "frothy barrier" of huge magnetic "bubbles," each of which is about 100 million miles across. A current hypothesis is that this "barrier" shields our solar system from much of the cosmic radiation in interstellar space.

Humanity First!

Each time mankind moves our horizons forward, we encounter new anomalies and infinite mysteries to unfold. One glaring anomaly is, why did it take so long to secure funding and an operational go-ahead for such an obviously valuable scientific endeavor as the New Horizons mission? Part of the answer lies in the fact that our nation has been under attack for decades by the cultural pessimism of the Anglo-Dutch oligarchy—and their economics of death—as well as the genocidal ide-

---

22. Other stellar systems with similar distributions of planets and belts have been discovered; most notably those orbiting Vega and Fomalhaut.

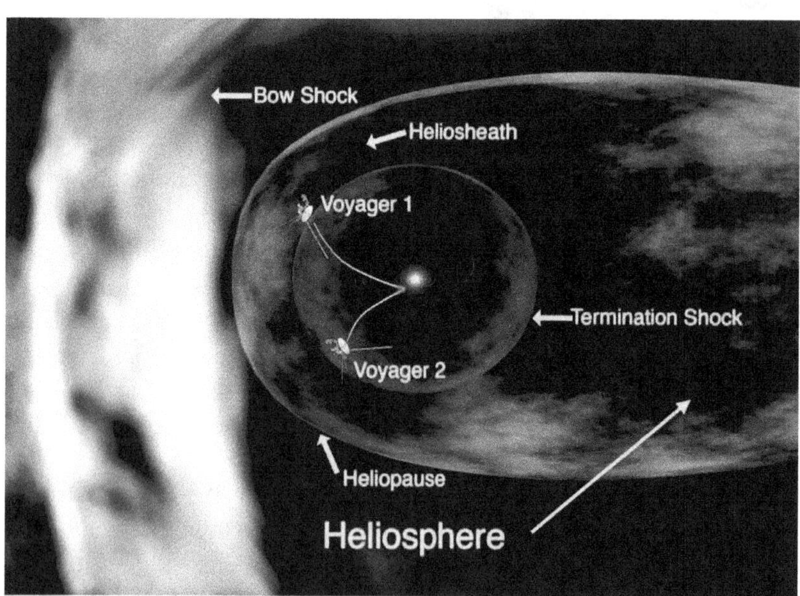

Artist's conception of the Heliosphere.

ology of the environmentalist movement. Your beliefs about the nature of man are a *political* factor; if you think that man is merely an animal, then you are enslaved more surely than with chains.

The other irony is that the NH scientists were able to execute this mission with such precision, so perfectly, and able to capture stupendous pictures of Pluto, yet these same scientists listen to rock music and adore science fiction, both of which are antithetical to creative thinking.[23] Even they operate within a fixed sphere, and wouldn't be capable of organizing the American people for a cultural Renaissance.

The future of space exploration for the United States is largely in the hands of "we the people." What has been holding us back in large degree, has been *subjective*. Most of the rest of humanity is now moving into a New Paradigm, a paradigm of optimism, as represented by the Silk Road/Belt and Road Initiative of China, which has been led and organized by Helga Zepp-LaRouche and the LaRouche political organization over the past several decades. It is time for America to join with those nations, bringing the best of our true culture to revitalize not only our basic industries, agriculture and infrastructure, but to uplift and inspire the minds of our youth to abandon the death culture of drugs and entropic thinking, and to once again, "reach for the stars."

Given the outpouring of enthusiastic public support for space exploration in general, and the New Horizons mission in particular, the American people have demonstrated that our deep cultural optimism can be revived with the appropriate leadership.[24] Were the present administration moved to openly support increased investment into space exploration, it would be welcomed by the American people.

America has led the way in space exploration, and it would benefit the world to experience increased cooperation amongst the scientific community in many nations toward the common goals of mankind. I encourage all scientists in America—no matter your specialty—to join with this New Paradigm, and passionately promote the development of a new economics, and a new astronomy for a renaissance of scientific and creative culture in America.

Mankind faces many challenges in our study of space; we have seen spectacular results from unmanned spacecraft in the exploration of the solar system. Imagine what we could do with a science based on Kepler, Leibniz and LaRouche. Imagine what we could do if LaRouche's Four Laws were implemented, and we saw a rebirth of true American System economics in the United States.

Isn't it time that we revive a *manned* space program in the United States? Isn't it high time that we go back to the Moon, and beyond?

For Further Reading

Follow the New Horizons spacecraft with NASA's app: https://eyes.nasa.gov

For more information about New Horizons: nasa.gov/mission_pages/newhorizons/main/index.html

Toward a Galactic Science Driver, a LaRouche PAC Scientific Team research report by Benjamin Deniston and Meghan Rouillard, *EIR* July 17, 2015.

Kepler, Johannes. *Harmonia Mundi* (Harmony of the World).

Kepler, Johannes, *Astronomia Nova* (The New Astronomy).

Leibniz, G.W.F., *Theodicy.*

---

23. The rock band Styx was invited to and toured the control center for the New Horizons mission.

24. According to Alan Stern, *thousands* of people showed up in person during the flyby to help celebrate the accomplishment; many millions followed it online, and the NASA website got so many hits that it crashed.

NOVEMBER 11, 2008

Only My Reforms Can Save The Planet from a Dark Age

by Lyndon H. LaRouche, Jr.

Lyndon LaRouche made the following remarks to a private meeting in Washington, D.C., on Nov. 11, 2008. The transcript has been edited, and subheads added.

As you know, probably, as of last July, I forecast that we were at the end of a phase of the system. And within three days, after my forecast, on July 25 of last year, the breakup of the present monetary system began, with what was called by some people who didn't know any better, a "subprime crisis." It was never a subprime crisis: The idea that a real estate bubble exploded and had a chain-reaction on the world is nonsense. That didn't happen: It happened the other way around.

The system which was to explode, or implode, just broke loose at its weakest point. But the problem lies, today, not in the real estate area or otherwise; it lies in financial derivatives. The financial derivatives system of the world is what is in the process of collapsing. And the financial derivatives system totals to over $1 quadrillion U.S. dollars in estimated value! And this is the great speculative bubble which has built up from 1987 on, under Alan Greenspan and others. This is the bubble that is now collapsing.

This is a hopeless collapse, in terms of the present system. *No mere reform of this present system, will*

EIRNS/Stuart Lewis

"We have an existential crisis on this planet," LaRouche told those gathered at a private meeting in Washington. He is shown here at a webcast on Oct. 1, 2008.

save the planet. The nearest event comparable to this, in all European civilization's experience, occurred in the 14th Century, with the general collapse, called a "New Dark Age," in which the entire system of Europe collapsed. The number of villages collapsed by one-half, the population of Europe collapsed by one-third, and it took several decades before even the beginning of civilization returned.

The crisis we have today, worldwide, is of a similar form: A great financial bubble, which has been growing at a great rate, while the rate of net physical production per capita, has been collapsing. This system is doomed in its present form. And there is no minor reform, there's no monetary reform that could save this system. We are headed for an *absolute, total collapse of the planet, unless a change is made*. There is no hope, for any remedy, within the framework of what's called a monetary system. But rather, as I shall emphasize here, the alternative is the establishment of a credit system, to replace the present monetary system.

JFK Library

Charles de Gaulle attempted to establish an American-style Presidential system in France, as against the European Parliamentary systems. He is shown here with U.S. President John F. Kennedy at the Elysée Palace in 1961.

The Crucial Role of the United States

Now, the model for the credit system lies in the United States, historically. If you study the U.S. Constitution and the peculiarities of the U.S. Constitution, as opposed to those of Europe, our system of government has no resemblance in essentials, to any European system of government. European systems of government are essentially parliamentary systems, not federal systems. There are reforms in European states, which have moved in the direction of a Presidential system. The best example of an attempt in that direction was Charles de Gaulle, as President of France, in his Fifth Republic. There was a serious attempt to establish a nation-state system in Europe, by de Gaulle. But since that time, there has been no successful effort, to establish a true nation-state system, as opposed to a parliamentary system.

Therefore, the United States has a crucial significance in this, and without a crucial role by the United States, which seems extremely difficult right now, because of the present Presidency and so forth—without the United States, there is no hope for avoiding what will be a plunge into a new dark age, resembling that which occurred in Europe, which occurred in the 14th Century. That's the situation we face. No simple reform, no adjustment, no monetary agreement, nothing of that sort will work.

There are, however, very specific measures, of agreements among governments which could change the system, could change it without anything too radical, but it would get us through.

Now, the first thing that has to happen is, in practice, is that unless there's an agreement of a certain type among the United States, Russia, China, and India, we have reached a condition, where it would be *impossible to save the world from a collapse*, a worldwide collapse. The form would be this: It would be the change of the present world monetary system, the elimination of the present world monetary system, to replace it by a credit system, which is consistent with the principles of the U.S. Federal Constitution. Remember that our Constitution, and our Presidential system, was not based on a parliamentary system; it was not based on a monetary system. It was based on what's called a credit system.

The difference is obvious to all of you: You have two types of systems in the world today, of any significance. One, there are credit systems: A credit means that the money issued by a government, is issued *by* a government, in the name of the government, and is backed by the promises of the government to support the credit. This credit, under law, can then be monetized and supply a money currency as well as credit for development.

This is distinct from a monetary system. A monetary system represents a system of money, which is *outside government*, but which may or may not have agreement *with* government. European systems, today, are not credit systems, they are monetary systems. The monetary system, which is tied to the IMF, today, and has been since 1971, 1972—that period—the monetary system is what is collapsing. The monetary system is collapsing, because it is tied, specifically now to the credit bubble, the derivatives bubbles. And this is what's collapsing. There's no possibility at this stage any longer, of saving the monetary system in its present form. That is, a reform made internal to the monetary system will not work. It's too late. We could have done something in that direction, back a year ago, July a year ago, back in 2007. The system is so rotten today, that it would not be possible, especially the changes that have been made by the U.S. and other governments, in the recent months, are so radical, that it would be impossible to reform this system. You have to completely overhaul it and revolutionize it.

But, our American System allows us to do that, under our Constitutional system in our history.

A Four-Power Agreement

Now, what we have to do is, is establish a power bloc, to force through a change among nations. Western Europe, despite the fact that there are positive elements, as the case of [Economics Minister Giulio] Tremonti in Italy, or some efforts on the part of [President Nicolas] Sarkozy in France; there are some initiatives in the direction of useful reforms. There are desires for useful reforms from other parts of the world. But the requirement here, is to have a sufficiently powerful agreement, *to force through* the reforms in a timely fashion. This can only occur by an agreement among the United States, Russia, China, and India. If the United States, Russia, China, and India function as a bloc, other countries will join them, and we can force through the reform. In my view, without that particular agreement, it would be impossible to ram through the reform, politically, at this time—not in time. We might eventually agree to it, but it would be too late. We need change now: The world system is collapsing at such a rate, now, that we do not have years to play with. We do not even have many months to play with. By the end of the year, we must be in the direction of making some kind of reform, in this direction.

Now, what it means, is this: As those of you from China know, and other countries, the change in the system, especially since 1971 and 1972 on, the change was a change in the relationship of China, from the United States to China and other countries. The change was essentially to what is called "globalization": to move production out of Europe and the United States, and to move it into countries which have low per-capita incomes: in other words, cheap labor. And thus production, and infrastructure, were moved *out* of the United States, and increasingly *out* of Europe, especially after 1989-1990, into other countries, Third World countries in particular, which operate at a cheap-labor price. Today, most of the production of the world depends critically, on a margin of production in these countries, which are the export countries, which replaced European production, U.S. production, and so forth.

So therefore, at this point, you have two things: First of all, the system is collapsing. Now, by the nature of the system, it means that the countries which were used as substitutes for production from Europe and the United States, for example, are now collapsing, because the purchases from other countries are collapsing, as in the case of China, where the collapse of China is a potential time-bomb for the entire planet. Because if the collapse of China's exports continues at the present rate, this will be a time-bomb for the entire system; and some people understand this. Therefore, the unity of four powers, the United States—which has a certain special power—Russia, China, and India, represents a bloc that can force through reforms of the type that are needed.

A Credit, Not a Monetary System

What is required is this: We have to eliminate the monetary system, by a credit system. A credit system is not some mysterious thing. It's essentially something which is traditional to the United States in particular. European systems today, are monetary systems: that is, despite agreements with government, money is controlled by agencies outside government. This is a characteristic of parliamentary systems—not a true Presidential system, but a parliamentary system. And thus, money exists *independently* of the control of government, although with agreement with government, but nonetheless, under the control of outside agencies: international, financial agencies, which actually control the monetary system, control and regulate the money, and government plays, less and less, a role in the control of money, in control of the monetary system. This is characteristic in Europe, particularly since 1989-1991, in which the control over money, with the Maastricht agreements and similar kinds of agreements, Europe has absolutely no control over its own monetary supply: It's controlled by outsiders, largely through London, and through things like the oil price market.

So therefore, the creation of a credit system to replace a monetary system, is where the solution lies. There's no way to save this monetary system in its present form. It's so full of junk, with the financial derivatives far in excess of a quadrillion dollars in claims, against the nominal size of the actual production of nations, it is impossible to reform this monetary system in its present form. You have to put the monetary system, itself, *through bankruptcy*. You will have to wipe out the greatest portion of nominal monetary assets in the world today! Cancel them! Because the system as a whole is hopelessly bankrupt.

Now, what do you do in that case? Well, what you do for a monetary reform to a credit system, you use the U.S. Constitution. Because of our Constitution, we can create, as Roosevelt did that formally, we can create a credit system. To replace a monetary system.

Now, what you do under this case, and with agreement with the United States, and its Constitution, with Russia, China, and India, it can be done. What you do, is you say, we put all the claims which are equivalent of monetary or credit claims in two piles. One pile we call "monetary." That's the manure pile. The other we call the "credit" pile. Now under the U.S. Constitution, money, when the Constitution is followed, is created only by the will of the government. It is done by the Executive branch of government, with the consent of the House of Representatives, and things flow from that. This credit being issued, is also authorized for monetization: So, the credit can be issued as loans for projects, or international loans, and part of it can actually be monetized, under the condition under which it was uttered. Particularly, if we had a national banking system, which we don't have presently, we could convert the Federal Reserve System, which is bankrupt,

White House/Shealah Craighead

About the time that President Bush was awarding Fed chairman Alan Greenspan the Presidential Medal of Freedom, in 2005 (shown here), Greenspan's galactic-size bubble, built up since 1987, had begun to burst.

into a national banking system, as Hamilton proposed. Then it would do that, automatically. We *do* need a national banking system in each country. That doesn't mean they're the only banks, but it does mean you use a national banking system to control the relationship between government and the banking system as a whole, in general.

Put the System Through Bankruptcy Reorganization

If you do that, then you do a bankruptcy reform: You take the hopelessly bankrupt system—we're talking about *quadrillions of dollars of claims*, of monetary claims, especially as located in these speculative markets of derivatives and related kinds of things—we have to wipe most of this off the books! It can never be paid. It was foolishness, it was a lie, it was done largely since 1987, under Alan Greenspan's insanity. This we have to wipe out.

What do you do? You have to protect those things which are productive, and are necessary for the government and necessary for the population. Therefore, you create a pile called the "credit pile." What you do, is you take every obligation, and every asset, which is valuable to society, currently, or necessary and meritorious—you take the monetary value of that, and you assign that to the creation of credit, government credit, a credit system. *And you leave the remainder to rot.*

Then, at that point, you enter into agreements, with governments—and this is where the relationship of the

United States, Russia, China, and India occurs; there are many ramifications to this thing—under the case, what we do first of all, is you create among these governments, and others who will join them, you create a credit system to replace the present monetary system. That doesn't mean that every nation is involved immediately; it means these nations and others who wish to join, will join immediately. Now, we enter into an agreement which amounts to a revival of the Bretton Woods system. What we do, therefore, is, we create a credit system, as an international system, as a *fixed-exchange-rate system.* And we issue credit, by agreement among these countries, as a fixed-exchange-rate system. We then proceed, to expand world production, involving these countries, *through* the new credit system, leaving the useless money, the useless claims, to rot.

ESA

Asia and Africa contain many of the raw materials assets required for the development of production around the world. The Brutish empire has prevent this development from taking place. Shown: the Palabora copper mine, Pretoria, South Africa.

In doing that, two things happen, particularly with these countries involved, because the future of the planet, economically, is concentrated in Asia, where the greatest single concentration of population and the need for growth exists. The other area, which has a similar character, is Africa. Now, Asia and Africa are also two areas, which contain a lot of the raw materials assets required for the development of production in the world.

Therefore, if this part of the world develops, several things happen: First of all, you have in China, and you have in India, and other countries in Asia, you have a tendency where 60-70% of the population is essentially destitute, because of the present structure of prices, prices paid. A small part of the population of these countries, varying from case to case, has, shall we say, a modern standard of living, a modern ability to produce. A great part of the population remains outside! While there's infrastructure development in China, it is not sufficient to compensate, for example, for these needs. The development of resources for developing raw materials, that is, mineral raw materials, is not sufficient. The raw materials, the minerals, lie there in the ground, but you just can't extract them, you have to develop these resources. And you have to mobilize the flow of this into the expansion of production to include

that: India, China, are typical of this—but also all of Asia.

You have a parallel situation in Africa. Africa is one of the larger repositories of raw materials, necessary for humanity in the coming period. But under the present conditions, with the lack of infrastructure, you can not develop those raw materials! So therefore, what you have, is a part of the world, over 40% of the world in Asia, essentially, and a large part in Africa, and you have comparable situations in South America, where you have large resources, which are undeveloped, which could be developed, but the infrastructure development needed, has not occurred yet.

The Challenge of Development

So therefore, we have not only the question of a reform of a monetary system, to prevent a collapse of the system; we have the challenge now, of taking these areas of development, which involve large raw materials deposits, at the same time, a very large part of the population—and a large part of the population of the world is living at substandard conditions, with no immediate prospect of significant improvement—therefore, the frontier of humanity, for centuries yet to come, involves this thrust of development. It means, then, a *reversal* of the present tendencies in Europe and in North America, away from becoming post-industrial societies, toward playing a key supporting role in freshly generating technologies which will support this development in Asia and in Africa, and also similarly, in South America. But South America's much closer to the United States, and so forth, has largely a European cultural population, and therefore, dealing with that is much different than it is in dealing with other parts of the world which have a different cultural heritage.

So therefore, there are two things involved: First of all, is to mobilize a section of the planet, which can be mobilized, which *has* to be mobilized—Russia knows it needs to mobilize! Russia is facing an existential crisis, not as severe as China's right now, but it's an existential crisis. They can not simply continue to function the way they're going. Changes are required. China knows that a change is required, from the present situation. India is less unstable in some respects than China, because its characteristics are different, but all of Asia is in this condition. Africa's in a *known* condition. The problem in South America, even though it's a different part of the world, and has different characteristics, is similar.

So therefore, we have to think not merely about a monetary reform, or a credit reform: We have to think of a credit reform in terms of a mission-orientation, of a system of sovereign nation-states, globally, for an extended period to come. Automatically, in this kind of process, if you have this agreement of the type I've indicated, among the four leading nations, and those who join them immediately, you will go immediately to a gold-denominated, fixed-exchange-rate system. So you will begin to operate in one part of the world, even if the rest of the world has not yet joined; you'll be operating under treaty agreements, among a bloc of nations, a powerful bloc of nations in these terms. And you're moving back in the direction we have to get, to solve these problems: a fixed-exchange-rate system.

What we would do, *probably*, and I would do in the United States, if I had my druthers, is take the Federal Reserve System, which is now bankrupt; the Federal Reserve System is hopelessly bankrupt. I say it: It's true. Merely, the axe has not the head off, yet, but it's gone! What you have to do, is put *it* through bankruptcy reorganization. Now, since it has a Federal government relationship, which the Federal government has to deal with, you simply do what Alexander Hamilton would have done, and intended to do, had he had his choices, despite Andrew Jackson—and convert the Federal Reserve System, as a set of assets, and use the power of government by an Act of Congress, and the Executive branch, to convert it into a National Bank. That does not mean it's the bank that controls everything in the banking system. You are going to restore the private banks, the state banks, and the Federal banks, the chartered banks. But you need a vehicle interfacing between government and the Treasury Department, and the private part of the banking system, to mediate the handling of long-term agreements, and the handling of other things which are done on behalf of *both* government interest and on the part of the institutions.

So, if we create this seed crystal, of these four nations, and others who join them, we now can have, any time we decide to do it—if the President of the United States says, to the President of Russia and to the President of China, and to the government of India, and some other countries: "Let's make this agreement!", the United States has Constitutionally, the Constitutional apparatus and the authority, to do this! So we don't have to worry about what somebody in England says, or some other part of the world says—if these countries agree, on a certain mission-orientation, to act now, we can start a process toward a recovery of the planet as a whole. And once we start that process, we then can go on to the major business of getting other parts of the world involved in it. But we need to make a break.

The American Presidential System

Now, we have, of course, a new President-elect of the United States, and provided he lives—I understand there are some threats to his life—the prospects don't seem good on the surface from his behavior, but if forces like that combine, the way the American Presidential system works, the President of the United States will be *shaped* by the approach to such an agreement. Sometimes a President determines the way the U.S. government goes, sometimes he does not. Sometimes he dominates, in a bad way. Sometimes he dominates in a good way. But our system is not a system of a President; it is a *Presidential system*, in which the entirety of the Federal government is essentially a Presidential system in its character. And the other branches of government are essentially auxiliary to our control-mechanism, which determine and shape the Presidency.

But if the United States Presidency decides to move in that direction, the forces of the Presidency can control the President of the United States. And therefore, the President of the United States will be inclined and steered to do useful things, for the sake of

EIRNS/Stuart Lewis

Our system, LaRouche stated, is not a system of a President; it is a Presidential *system, which involves the entirety of the Federal government. Shown: President-elect Obama campaigning in Leesburg, Va., Oct. 22, 2008.*

the United States and for its allies. So that's what's required.

If we do that, then we can deal with other parts of the world, which eagerly join. The problem now, is the attempt to pick off one country at a time, to agree with this—the kind of negotiations that are occurring between London and Sarkozy of France, is completely hopeless! Nothing good can come out of this! It's absolutely useless. And the results we'll see, in the coming meeting [the Nov. 15 G-20 meeting—ed.], will be terrible results. They'll be inconsequential; it'll be chaotic. *No solution will be presented!* Something may be presented and called a "solution." But, calling a pig a person does not make it human. This will not work.

Nothing presently planned, by the coming meeting, will do any damned good, at all—but will only make things worse. Only a reform of the type I've described, is within sight as a feasible change in the system.

What I've said, also implies that we would go away from a floating-exchange-rate system, not only to a gold-reserve system, or a regulated system of the type that Roosevelt prescribed in 1944, as opposed to what Truman did after 1945: What Truman did, what was done under Truman, was not Roosevelt's intention. Remember, that Franklin Roosevelt's intention was to

eliminate all imperialism, to get rid of colonialism, and to use the vast economic power we had assembled in the war, to build up other countries, through a partnership to eliminate colonialism, and to establish a system of nation-states on this planet.

Truman was different: Truman was actually an enemy, a political enemy of Franklin Roosevelt. He belonged to a different faction, an opposing faction. Roosevelt died. Truman took over—in a sense, Winston Churchill took over. And if President Roosevelt, who had intended to *eliminate* colonialism throughout the planet, through a process of development, was replaced by a President who cooperated with the British to *restore colonialism*—as in the case in Indochina, as in the case in Indonesia, and so forth and so on, around the planet.

So what happened under Truman, was *not* the actual intention of Roosevelt. If we go back to 1944, at Bretton Woods—against Keynes! Keynes was a fascist and an imperialist! That's frankly what he was; his famous 1937 *General Theory*, published in Berlin, in which he said his system would work better in Nazi Germany than it would in a free country. He was right. The Keynesian system was adapted to a colonial/imperial system, and we functioned under a monetarist system, with imperialistic characteristics, especially since 1971 to the present time: It's been one of our big problems.

So, going back to the *Roosevelt* intention, of 1944-early 1945, with a reform of this type, does give us an answer. This means that we have to have a fixed-exchange-rate system; we have to have a hard-currency system; it means we have to have a lot of regulation of prices. You can not have free, floating prices. Because, if you're not covering the costs of production, by undercutting prices, so that you try to produce below the cost of production, you're not going to have development.

The World Needs Infrastructure

This also means, that this will not work without a very large-scale investment in basic economic infrastructure. For example: Take the case of Asia, North Asia.

North Asia is a repository, part of Russia, but North

National Archives

Franklin Roosevelt's intention was to eliminate all imperialism and colonialism, and to use the vast economic power the United States had assembled during the war, to build up other countries, and to establish a system of nation-states. FDR is shown here with President Edwin Barclay of Liberia, January 1943.

Asia in general; the Siberian area and below, is a repository of concentration of raw materials which are necessary for the development of Asia as a whole. But you just can't go in there, and get those raw materials; you have to have a system of development, which develops the territory in which the raw materials lie. You can't just go down and dig them out. You have to have a system, and Russia used to have a system of that type, under the old Russian system, in infrastructure, in minerals. And therefore, to develop this area, you require large-scale, modern transportation systems; you need power systems, which means nuclear power systems, and so forth; otherwise you can not develop these territories. This means developing magnetic levitation systems in place of rail systems, restoring rail systems where they fit the bill, and all other kinds of infrastructural development which are necessary for high-technology investment and production. Without that, we can not accomplish our mission.

Therefore, we have to have very large-scale international agreements on creation of credit, for large-scale infrastructure projects, of especially international interest. You can do nothing in Africa, without a large investment in basic economic infrastructure: mass transportation, power, water management, and so forth. These countries, given freedom—true freedom—could tend to develop themselves. *But!* Without large-scale infrastructure, which they're not equipped to develop, they couldn't launch that kind of development.

This means, also, the world itself, at large, requires a return to large-scale rail or magnetic levitation transportation systems, which we've been destroying in the post-war period. It means other kinds of development of that type.

It means also, a new tariff system, a protectionist system, which guarantees to each nation, that its investment in production, which everybody has supported, presumably, is going to be protected in price. We can not have a low-price economy. The problem in China, for example, is, the prices at which China is able to have an export market, the prices are too low! You can not maintain China's population with those prices. And the reason this was done, was to lower the price of production below the *cost* of production! So we moved production *out* of Europe, and out of North America, we moved it to prices *below the actual, physical cost of production*, considering the capital investment in technology. Therefore, you take and dump on China and other countries, you dump an export market for them, but then you don't allow them to earn enough to support their entire population in development. The same thing happens in Africa. The same thing has happened in South America and Central America, in recent periods, mainly since the 1970s.

So we need these kinds of reforms, now! And that's the direction we have to go in. That's the option.

Billions Are Already Imperiled

If we're not willing to move in the direction I've indicated here, in these remarks so far, today, then, I tell you, that the situation for humanity on the planet as a whole is worse today, than it was in Europe in the 14th Century, in the onset of what was called the New Dark Age. We have over 6.5 billion people living on this planet today. With the present conditions, much of that population is already imperiled: the question of food supplies, alone, problems of disease and related things; the food crisis is grave on this planet, today, as many of us know: Without an increase in productivity, *physical productivity*, which means a change in these conditions, and the introduction of protectionist conditions, we're going to have a holocaust. We now have between 6.5 and 7 billion people on this planet: If we don't do something now, we're going to end up, in a couple of generations, with about 1 billion, or less.

So, we have an existential crisis on this planet. The present monetary system, the present systems, especially since 1968-71/72, the *net physical output of the United States, since 1968,* since the fiscal year of '67-'68—the net physical output per capita of the United States *has been continually shrinking! There has been no net physical growth, per capita, per square kilometer, in the United States since fiscal year '67-'68.*

You have a similar condition, but a worse condition, in Europe today, especially in Germany: In Germany, the most obvious collapse has occurred.

So, if these reforms are not made, with the goal of a protectionist system, which ensures that long-term investment is promoted and encouraged, and technological progress and the investment that goes with it, is encouraged, *we are headed—right now—for a new dark age!* Not some time down the line. What has happened, at an accelerating rate, since the end of July of 2007, has already been a run into a crisis.

One of the problems here, is that every economist who engages in forecasting has failed, in this entire period. They failed in the long term, but they've also failed, in particular in the past year and a half. Every economist in the world, that I know of, has been generally incompetent in forecasting, during this period. Incompetent, particularly—you have people who are publishing reports to the effect that this crisis will soon be over. It will never be over! Without this reform I've indicated, it will never be over! Life on this planet is headed for a dark age, unless the kind of reforms I've indicated occur now. There *is* no other solution. And

KCI Konecranes

If the U.S., Russia, China, and India agree to establish a New Bretton Woods system, other nations, such as Japan and South Korea, will leap to the chance to join them. Shown: Enormous cranes at a port in South Korea.

any forecaster who says differently, you know is incompetent.

And that's why I say—I return to it—the key to a reform, as I see it today: There's no possibility of a necessary reform, unless you reach agreement of the United States, Russia, China, and India. If those countries agree on the general directions I indicate, and are prepared to act in that direction, other nations will join them—obviously, Japan will join them, automatically! Korea will automatically join them! Other countries will immediately join them, because they're part of the same system, the East Asian system. That whole area of East Asia, Northern Siberia, the area around Korea, the same thing—these are areas that have *immediate* potential for very significant development! And these countries, given the chance, will leap to that, and take advantage of that.

But without that kind of reform, without that orientation, without agreements where we can create large masses of *new credit*—that is, under a credit system, while junking the old monetary system—if we can't do that, there's no chance for humanity at all. And anyone who forecasts differently is *wrong, and dangerously wrong.*

If we don't make this kind of reform now, we're not going to have a decent planet to live on for some time to come.

Worse than 'Fake News': The Forced Conformity of the Media!

by Helga Zepp-LaRouche, Chairwoman of the
German political party Büso, the Civil Rights Solidarity Party

The following is an English translation of an article appearing in the German newspaper, Neue Solidarität.

Aug. 4—We should have learned from the 1920s and 1930s that the spread of cultural pessimism throughout the population has fatal consequences. But such pessimism is spreading today in many Western societies, and especially in Germany, in the face of uncertain future options, with the result that more and more citizens have completely given up the hope of being able to make a difference through their own participation, or they are joining right-wing parties that provide an outlet for anger but offer no solutions. The culprit in this development is not least the political establishment, which leads us to accept a "TINA" politics—TINA is the acronym for "there is no alternative"—and the forced conformity of the mainstream media, which suppress all messages that point to alternatives.

EDITORIAL

We are living through what is probably the greatest strategic change of all time. Under the leadership of the BRICS countries (Brazil, Russia, India, China, and South Africa), the majority of the developing countries are currently focussing on close win-win cooperation, with the aim of achieving the leap to the status of industrialized nations, and a good standard of living for their entire populations as quickly as possible. The 10th BRICS Summit in Johannesburg July 25-27 included some of the largest and most important international organizations of developing countries, such as the Group of 77, the Organization of Islamic Cooperation (OIC), Mercosur, and the African Union, which were there to join forces with the BRICS in what might be called the Global South initiative.

The New Silk Road Is Changing Everything

China's Belt and Road Initiative, and the idea that relations are no longer based on geopolitical confrontation but on mutual benefit, have changed the political climate in many regions of the world in a completely positive way. For example, the election victory of newly designated Pakistani Prime Minister Imran Khan has created for the first time the potential to settle the conflict between India and Pakistan. Khan promised to ensure that his country takes two steps toward India for every step that India takes towards Pakistan. The cooperation between the BRICS countries also has its impact on Pakistan; China has traditionally good relations with Pakistan, and just now the Russian and Pakistani navies had a high-level meeting, after the first-ever joint manoeuvres of Russian and Pakistani ground troops took place just one year ago.

The Horn of Africa is also embraced by the new spirit of cooperation. There the hitherto mutually hostile states of Somalia, Djibouti, Eritrea and Ethiopia are massively expanding their mutual diplomatic and economic relations, largely thanks to Chinese investment, such as in the construction of the railway from Djibouti to Addis Abeba.

And, in contrast to the consistently negative media coverage of the progress of negotiations between North and South Korea and the United States, this process is on a good track, with the option that a leading North Korean government official may speak in New York before the upcoming UN General Assembly in September.

Meanwhile, the Syrian government has begun the economic reconstruction of the province of Aleppo. The first part of a three-phase program is the reconstruction of the infrastructure, the second step is the specific provisioning of each individual family, and the third phase is the return of people to a safe environment, as the Deputy Governor of the province, Hamid Kenno, stressed. At the same time, the Russian military has helped create a refugee center in Syria that will welcome refugees returning from Jordan, Lebanon, and Turkey, and assist them in their return to their homes. An interministerial coordination committee of the Russian Foreign and Defense Ministries has taken over the orderly repatriation of the refugees.

You Aren't Hearing the Good News

One might assume that these developments would dominate headlines, immediately bringing hope to all clear-thinking people that world peace has become more secure, poverty can be overcome, and the refugee crisis can be resolved in a human way. Instead, the media do not say a word about the "Global South" initiative. An article in the German national daily, *Die Welt*, furnished with much geopolitical spin, cites Xi Jinping's speech at the BRICS Summit: "Africa has more development potential than any other region in the world." And what does the author conclude? That "China is working to build its empire" and the upcoming summit between China and the African nations in Beijing this September is just Xi Jinping's "charm offensive."

Of course, this censorship of good news has the purpose of depicting the politics of the old neo-liberal paradigm as having no alternative. If China—incidentally, along with India, Russia and Japan—now demonstrates that Africa can indeed be industrialized, and if that were truthfully reported, then someone might think to ask why the African continent, after centuries of colonialism and decades of the IMF's notorious credit conditionalities, is in its current precarious state, and whether this is not a major cause of the refugee crisis.

Instead of responding to China's repeated offer to work together with the African states on their industrialization in the context of the New Silk Road, the German government is blocking Chinese investments in Germany, such as the recent acquisition of the precision machinery manufacturer Leifeld Metal Spinning, although various surveys confirm that Chinese investors have always taken care to increase the number of jobs and raise wages. Where was the government's veto when, in recent years, dozens of American and British hedge funds have taken everything from mid-sized companies to housing companies and infrastructure, carved out the choicest portions to sell, and closed down the rest as socially unacceptable?

It is an absurd idea to think that one could halt the rise of emerging and developing countries—India and China alone account for 2.6 billion people—and impose the neo-liberal model of geopolitics as the only possible option on the rest of the world. Blair's and Obama's policies of converting the whole world to Western democracy through regime change and "humanitarian" interventions, as a sort of modern crusade, have clearly failed. Neither China nor Russia wants this model, and more and more developing countries see the Chinese model as the model for their own development.

The reason is that the BRICS offer a form of cooperation that focuses on mutual development, while "the West" prefers the neo-liberal model of profit maximization for the few at the expense of the many. It is also not overlooked in the rest of the world that the EU is slipping into more and more disagreement between its member states, whether in dealing with the refugee crisis; in choosing between greater integration versus emphasis on sovereignty; or in relations with China, Russia and the United States.

Looking at the world through Eurocentric glasses obscures the view that the greater part of humanity, represented by the BRICS and Global South, has drawn from the neo-liberal policies of the West the conclusion that a revision of the current system of global governance is urgently needed, and that this reorganization cannot be left to the West.

Instead of arrogantly continuing to sit on the high horse of egoism in their supposed superiority and soon landing their own populations on the margins of history, the nations of Europe, and the United States, should look to the offers from China and Russia for co-operation and co-creation of the New Paradigm. Despite the punitive tariffs imposed by Trump, China continues to offer cooperation with the United States in order to overcome the trade deficit through joint ventures in third countries. A spokeswoman for China's Ministry of Commerce has just said, "We always believe that bad things can be turned into good ones and challenges can be turned into opportunities."

And at the just-ended ASEAN Summit in Singapore, Russian Foreign Minister Lavrov recalled Putin's words at the 2016 Russia-ASEAN Summit in Sochi, where he called on partner-countries to be aware of the huge geopolitical and geo-economic potential of the Eurasian continent, where the Eurasian Economic Union (EAEU), the Shanghai Corporation Organization (SCO) and Association of Southeast Asian Nations (ASEAN) complement each other. Lavrov stressed that the door remains open to the EU, and no one should doubt that the EU should be interested in it purely for pragmatic economic and business interests.

But one could also find reasons for such cooperation that go beyond the pragmatic. If Europe does not want to completely forget, and lose, its humanistic and classical culture, then we could revive the ideas of Nicholas of Cusa, Leibniz and Schiller, and make our contribution to the development of humanity. You certainly will not read about it in the mainstream media. But you can read it here.

zepp-larouche@eir.de

Are You a Dupe for British Dope? Marijuana Effectively Legalized in New York City

by Diane Sare

Aug. 5—As of August 1, 2018, New York District Attorney Cyrus Vance, Jr. has mandated that marijuana possession and use are no longer considered criminal acts in New York County (Manhattan).

If you believe that this is a good thing, you have already lost your mind. Hopefully, you are still able to muster the attention span required to consider for a moment the possibility that you are terribly, terribly wrong.

Although Vance's action does not have the authority of state law, the order to end all prosecutions effectively makes the use of marijuana *de facto* legal. This follows on the heels of the complete legalization of "recreational" use of marijuana in Colorado, California, Alaska, Maine, Oregon, Massachusetts, Nevada and Washington state—all of this in direct defiance of Federal statutes which classify cannabis as a Schedule I drug under the federal Controlled Substances Act of 1970.

It has now been fifty years since Lyndon LaRouche warned in the 1960s that the emergence and toleration of the "rock, drug, sex counter-culture" would lead to the destruction of the United States. What was then the "counter-culture" has now become "popular culture." Ask yourself: was LaRouche correct? Have we been destroyed?

On the one hand, we now inhabit a nation where hundreds of Americans commit suicide on a daily basis; a nation where tens of thousands of talented young Americans die every year of opioid overdoses; a nation where tent cities and homeless encampments are be-coming commonplace in urban areas; a nation where tens of millions of Americans seek escape from the pain and carnage of everyday life through anti-anxiety, anti-depressant and other prescription medications.

We also inhabit a nation where massive areas of land, housing cumulatively millions of people, are now engulfed in fire or flood due to lack of investment in basic water management infrastructure; a nation which has still not rebuilt the areas devastated by numerous hurricanes and storms, going all the way back to Katrina; a nation where life expectancy is declining, the death rate is increasing and tens of millions suffer under inadequate health care.

Over the past fifty years America has been destroyed by the murderous financial and economic policies that have flowed from the City of London and Wall Street. In the midst of this, what is the message coming from the pro-drug crowd? Can't find a job? Can't exist on the minimum wage? Can't afford to rent an apartment? Can't afford to have children or raise them properly? Stuck in an existence which is going nowhere? Relax! Relax, and light up a joint. Get high—and maybe play a video game while you're at it. If your troubles still exist tomorrow, well, just fire up another joint!

The legalization of drugs plays the same precise role it played 175 years ago in the British Opium Wars against China: to keep people who are being economically exploited servile and stupid—and to entice those same people to stupidly embrace their own servility, their own slavery. Drugs are a means for the conscious self-oppression of the population. If this is tolerated, then America is finished as a nation.

This is the critical juncture at which your own personal responsibility arises. It is not enough that YOU don't smoke marijuana. This is absolutely not an issue of "personal choice." Your toleration of the legalization of drugs is itself almost a criminal act, for if drugs are legalized, the nation which gave birth to you, educated you and gave you opportunity—the nation which millions fought and died to defend—will be destroyed. You have no right as a citizen to allow that to happen.

The Destruction of the Human Identity

The actual issue we are confronted with, in the widespread support for the legalization of drugs, is that the majority of our people have lost all understanding of what it means to be a human being. To be very explicit: the survival of human beings depends entirely on our ability to think! If we cannot think, we will not survive! People who are on drugs cannot think properly. They may think they can; they may insist—angrily—that they can. But they can't. This is true in the very acute case, like someone driving an 18-wheeler 80 mph while high; but it is more true, and more devastating for the species as a whole to lose the ability to make and assimilate a scientific discovery when the survival of the species depends upon it. Do you think that a bunch of people smoking dope are going to figure out how to stop an asteroid from hitting the planet? Do you think these same dopers will find a cure for cancer, or discover how to travel to remote planets and galaxies? A society which tolerates the destruction of the creative potential of its citizenry will never do any of these things. That is why legalizing drugs must be considered a crime against humanity.

Take the case of our present culture which is built around the worship of money and monetary values, as a measure of economic success. Earlier generations understood that a successful economy must be based on physical-economic production, and this requires revolutions in physical economy, energy production and transportation. Today, it is difficult to get people to even think in physical-economic terms. People who support solar energy and oppose nuclear power or people who support "bicycle lanes" but oppose high-speed rail, are people who have lost their ability to think rationally about economics and science. They think they think. But they don't think—at least not above the level of a baboon. And this is all the product of fifty years of increasing drug use in the country.

Take also the case of the British-run environmentalist movement, a crucial part of the "rock, drug, sex counter-culture." The trans-Atlantic oligarchy has spent billions of dollars over the last 60 years to convince you that there is no difference between a human being and an animal. In fact, they argue that beasts are superior to humans. Yet, it is the same elites who enforce policies of brutal economic austerity who finance the environmentalist movement, as well as the push for drug legalization. Why? Because they are determined to eradicate human creativity, human discovery and scientific and technological progress. They desire to run the world as one giant Malthusian plantation, just as the British Empire ran India and her African colonies. Keep the natives backward. Keep them stupid. Keep them drugged.

And young Americans, those who have not yet killed themselves through suicide or drug overdose— what do they do? They are instructed to support a "Green Agenda," to "Save the Planet," to stop "dirty" industry and "dangerous" nuclear power, all the while toking away.

In the history of the Planet Earth, 99 percent of all animal and plant species have become extinct. They suffered this fate because they could not change! They could not discover new principles of science and economics which allowed them to transform their relationship with nature. Only humans can accomplish that. That is what it means to be human.

Let's take one simple example that Lyndon LaRouche has cited on numerous occasions: human beings cook their food. This seemingly simple act alone must have increased the average lifespan dramatically, by reducing disease and pestilence found in decomposing flesh. Who made the first fire? We will never know; and it's likely that fire was brought into use by different groups of people in different locations, but what we do know, is that the use of fire in cooking was not a result of a genetic permutation. That is, the first person to ignite a fire did not have any physical features that other people did not possess. Discovering the use of fire was not a function of having a longer or shorter nose, or arms, or whether one was left or right-handed. The discovery of a new principle, which can transform the entire universe, occurs uniquely, and willfully, inside the mind of a human being. Human beings also are capable of forming societies where such discoveries can become integrated into the behavior of the species as a whole, thus making it possible for them to live longer and transform their mode of existence. Human beings are able to improve their species at will!

Ending the Scourge

What is required is a War on Drugs, precisely as Lyndon LaRouche formulated in a March 9, 1985 speech, "A Proposed Multi-National Strategic Operation against the Drug Traffic for the Western Hemisphere," to an anti-drug conference in Mexico City. What is required is Total War, one into which every person reading this editorial should enlist.

The people pushing the legalization of drugs are the ones who run the drug trade already! People like George Soros and the Koch Brothers already have made their fortunes through speculation and money laundering, with murderous results. Now, through legalization, they seek to turn your children into drug-addicted, suicidal, homicidal zombies. It is no coincidence that these are the same individuals who are to be counted among the fiercest enemies of President Donald Trump.

Some among you may have bought into the ridiculous argument that the legalization of drugs will "reduce crime" or increase government revenues through taxation. Those arguments come from the drug pushers themselves. Ask yourself, has the legalization of gambling reduced crime? Have the revenues from it improved our schools, our health care, or built needed infrastructure? Don't be a dupe. Wall Street and London oligarchs want to legalize drugs to enslave us. That is the only issue.

Others among you insist that a War on Drugs is "racist." Again, don't be a dupe. The minority populations in America were deliberately targeted with drugs to destroy the movement of Martin Luther King, to make people servile and obedient. Remember the almost military-style saturation of the inner cities with Crack some years ago? The legalization of drugs will *increase* drug usage among minorities. Is that what you want? Will legalization of drugs stop racism? Will it stop people from being pulled over for "driving while Black?" No! Drug legalization goes hand-in-hand with economic policies which will further impoverish the population, leading to more crime, more incarcerations, more hopelessness. This is why Barack Obama's pro-drug-legalization outlook is so despicable.

The only solution to this scourge is to shut down Dope Inc.—to destroy completely the financial and banking nexus that stands behind the inter-locking regime of financial speculation, drug trafficking, and economic looting. This will require fundamental changes in economic and banking policies. A critical first step must be re-enactment of Franklin Roosevelt's Glass-Steagall legislation, to clean out the speculation and money laundering mess. At the same time the United States should begin negotiations with other nations for a return to a global system of fixed exchange rates, as Lyndon LaRouche has proposed in his call for a New Bretton Woods conference. This all must occur within a shift back into technologically progressive investment and increased funding for advanced scientific enterprises, such as NASA and fusion energy research. All of this is contained in the economic recovery proposal put forward by Lyndon LaRouche in 2014, "Four New Laws to Save the U.S.A. Now!"

The American people have been through 50 years of degradation; they have accommodated themselves to a bestial standard of culture and behavior. But, Americans are also human, and as Lyndon LaRouche put it in his 2004 study, "On the Subject of Tariffs and Trade,"

> … despite those excursions into depravity, we have, until now, remained, genetically, in the political sense of the term, what [Benjamin] Franklin's legacy made us…. Our Constitution, and our conception of an anti-British East India Company policy known as the American System of Political Economy, our fundamental opposition to an intrinsically predatory and imperialist Anglo-Dutch Liberalism, is a deeply embedded special character, our patriotic tradition, even today.

It is that patriotic character which we must call upon today to bring ourselves and our fellow Americans back to our right minds. You can only call yourself a citizen if you are engaged in this battle. The ruling of Cyrus Vance, Jr. must be rescinded! New Yorker Alexander Hamilton's ghost is warning you: Don't be a slave of the British!